Healing
Heal Your Mind, Heal Your Body

Change Your Life

2nd Edition

2nd Edition

By Mary Solomon

© **Copyright 2015 – Mary Solomon - All rights reserved.**

In no way is it legal to reproduce, duplicate, or transmit any part of this document in either electronic means or in printed format. Recording of this publication is strictly prohibited and any storage of this document is not allowed unless with written permission from the publisher. All rights reserved.

The information provided herein is stated to be truthful and consistent, in that any liability, in terms of inattention or otherwise, by any usage or abuse of any policies, processes, or directions contained within is the solitary and utter responsibility of the recipient reader. Under no circumstances will any legal responsibility or blame be held against the publisher for any reparation, damages, or monetary loss due to the information herein, either directly or indirectly.

Respective authors own all copyrights not held by the publisher.

Legal Notice:

This eBook is copyright protected. This is only for personal use. You cannot amend, distribute, sell, use, quote or paraphrase any part or the content within this eBook without the consent of the author or copyright owner. Legal action will be pursued if this is breached.

Disclaimer Notice:

Please note the information contained within this document is for educational and entertainment purposes only. Every attempt has been made to provide accurate, up to date and reliable complete information. No warranties of any kind are expressed or implied. Readers acknowledge that the author is not engaging in the rendering of legal, financial, medical or professional advice.

By reading this document, the reader agrees that under no circumstances are we responsible for any losses, direct or indirect, which are incurred as a result of the use of information contained within this document, including, but not limited to, —errors, omissions, or inaccuracies.

CONTENTS

INTRODUCTION

SECTION 1: THE WORKINGS OF THE MIND AND THE BODY

CHAPTER 1 – THE WAY THE MIND AND BODY WORK IN HARMONY

CHAPTER 2 – HEALING THE MIND

CHAPTER 3 – LISTENING TO YOUR BODY

CHAPTER 4 - LEARNING NOT TO BE A MARTYR

SECTION 2: CONVENTIONAL METHODS OF HEALING

CHAPTER 5 – EXERCISES IN MINDFULNESS

CHAPTER 6 – MAKING YOUR LIFE HAPPY

CHAPTER 7 – SPOILING YOURSELF

CHAPTER 8 – EMBRACING POSITIVE CREATIVITY

CHAPTER 9 – WORKING YOUR WAY THROUGH MENTAL AND PHYSICAL PAIN

CHAPTER 10 – HEALING THROUGH MEDITATION

CHAPTER 11 – HEALING THROUGH YOGA

SECTION 3: THE UNCONVENTIONAL METHODS OF HEALING

CHAPTER 12 – HEALING THROUGH THE LAW OF ATTRACTION

CHAPTER 13 – HEALING THROUGH CHAKRAS

CHAPTER 14 – HEALING THROUGH SELF – HYPNOSIS

CHAPTER 15 – HEALING USING CRYSTALS

CONCLUSION

Introduction

It is becoming more and more recognized by science and by medicine that the way that individuals feel is largely dictated by the thoughts that they have. For example, two people with the same illness may see it very differently. One may be very sick indeed because of the way that the mind perceives that illness, while the other may appear to be accepting of the illness and yet making such strides in their life as to be extraordinary. The difference between the perceptions of human beings is vast and it's complex.

This book is written because your life is worth it. If you really do want to heal your mind, heal your body and change your life, then the book has a great deal of substance and will help you to achieve that. You are seeking answers and that's what brought you here, but within the pages of this book, the answers are put in a plain and easy to understand manner so that anyone can achieve that peace of mind and calm in their lives that they merit. We have but one life, and when that's filled to brimming with negativity, the mind and the health suffer.

Looking through the chapters you will learn all about being the master of your own life and being able to dictate and even predict your response to the bricks that life just happens to throw in your direction. Your mental aptitude, your approach to life in general and your ability to find inner strength depend upon understanding basic principles which are outlined within these pages to help you achieve your desires.

Why was the book so important to me, as an author? It was important that the words were written. There are so many guides on the market that purport to help by using fancy wording and technical psychobabble, and none of them helped me. Hardly what one would describe as a "new age" chick or guy, it seemed that there wasn't a book for down to earth people like me and that's a great shame. The people who are the average Joes are left behind on this voyage to inner discovery and they shouldn't be. This book addresses that in a very positive and practical way. Enjoy your journey.

Section 1: The workings of the mind and the body

Chapter 1 – The Way The Mind And Body Work In Harmony

People come up with all these solutions and toss them at you as if you can grasp complex workings easily. For example, yoga isn't just sitting on a mat posing in strange positions. It's complex. It takes different breathing techniques, exercises and self-discipline to try it and to gain any benefit. The mind and the body working together don't necessarily come as a natural process to everyone. For example, if you are unhappy, your body may become neglected because it takes second priority. People who have emotional problems may binge eat or may neglect the amount of sleep that they have. They may also surround themselves with negative ideas.

Similarly, the body can react to all kinds of actions that you take. Take a look at these and you will see what I mean:

- You watch too much TV at night
- You stay in bed too much
- You don't exercise
- You don't drink water
- You are too tempted by the wrong foods

We all know that we are doing these things, but we still keep doing them until the body can no longer be in harmony with the mind. The willpower has taken precedence over what the body needs. As a consequence, we look for labels. There are so many times that I hear people complain about ailments or conditions of their body, but who cannot see that if they corrected the treatment they subject their body to, that can all be reversed and the body can begin to heal.

There's an inner voice that is speaking to you every time you feel that your body needs something. This may be thirst, hunger, rest, exercise etc. Each of these are bodily needs and those who ignore them tend to want to place the blame squarely on life or some medical ailment that has a name. The problem is that by doing this, and hiding behind the medicines that they are given, they never actually heal the body and they don't change this mindset. Thus, there's absolutely no chance of them healing.

The mind and body work together. The mind has a creative side and an intellectual side. It also has a side that you may not think a lot about, but it's there anyway. This side of the mind is the subconscious. It is this side of the mind that needs to come out sometimes in order for perfect balance of body and mind. The time when this happens can be explained easily. Imagine you lose something and the more you think about it, the less likely you are to come up with the solution of where you placed that object. Your thoughts actually block your subconscious from helping you. Now think about how it came to you, out of the blue when you were not thinking about it, and you were able to find that object. The mind needed a little quietude so that the subconscious could do its work. It also needs sleep because the brain needs the healing power of sleep in order to feel refreshed and ready for another day. During this time of sleep, the subconscious is able to work on all the problems that you may have and come up with solutions all on its own without you consciously putting any effort in.

The mind is also powerful when it comes to healing, as can be proven by the placebo effect. This effect kicks in when someone believes that something will make him or her better. A child believes that a mother's kiss makes that sore leg better, and in the same way, the placebo effects doesn't just involve pills. If you believe that you can heal, you can. Thus, you can see that having the mind open to the possibility of self-healing is important.

The body, on the other hand, needs nourishment, exercise, rest and play in order to feel well and when it doesn't get any of these, it is likely to upset the balance between the mind and the body. People who don't sleep will not be able to cope as well as those that do. They feel sluggish and cannot perform to the same extent as those who do sleep for the required time. People who live on foods that are high in carbohydrates or sugars allow their mind a sugar rush, but instead of being a positive thing, what happens when the sugar rush is gone is that the body slows down and craves more sugar. The vicious circle of body and mind fighting each other to have their needs met is common.

In order to fight that cycle, the first steps are actually admitting that you have a problem and being absolutely sure that you want to go through the process of healing. Those who smoke, for example, may be sure they want to quit, but how addicted are they? Can they do it without help? Will they seek the help they need or dismiss it because it's easier? Those who diet starve their bodies of what it has become accustomed to in order to reach a goal, but when that goal is reached, they make the body even more sensitive to change of diet and go back to the old ways. We are our own worst enemy when it comes to actually taking responsibility for our mind and body connection.

So, before you dismiss this book entirely based on the fact that you want to smoke or eat excessively, the method described in the chapters that follow allow you to do whatever you want but to recognize what its doing and simply cut back a little to give your body and mind a better connection. Deprivation isn't necessary. What is necessary is finding out which ailments you have that is self-inflicted and which are beyond your control. When you begin this journey and deal with all of the hardships your mind gives your body, all of the ailments that are not of your making become easier to bear because your body is better equipped to deal with them.

Both psychological illness and physical illness can be caused by the way that people live their lives. For example, if you surround yourself with negativity, all you can expect from life is negativity. If you want to "change your life" as the title suggests, this means making changes in the way that you approach life and everyday problems and taking another route which maximizes your own personal potential. There is always going to be a huge difference between the way two people sees a half full cup, when there is a negative and positive attitude. The positive person sees a half full cup while the negative person sees a half empty one. That's because negativity and positivity affect the way you think.

So how do you make a change that will last a lifetime? This book is written especially for you because I have made a change. I know the difference between being happy and being extremely sad and want to pass that gift to you. As you begin to unwrap this gift, by acting in the ways suggested within the book's pages, you will begin to reap the benefits and, in the process, will feel the energy return to your life, so that you no longer feel you need healing.

Keeping to the lines shown in the book as a means to go forward, your lifestyle will give you more energy, more zest for life and less illness and emotional turmoil. Taking off the final ribbons on that gift, you will find that your life is more valuable to you than it ever has been before and you will begin to see that your life is indeed something that has changed for the better.

Chapter 2 – Healing The Mind

This journey may take you a little bit of time to get used to. The exercises suggested here are to help your mind to think of things that positively reinforce healing. In this day and age, we believe that stress has to be part of our lives because it is. However, when you train your mind in the ways suggested, you begin to free up space within your mind, which in turn allows you to feel better about whom you are.

Imagine this scenario. You are very angry with your child for not doing as he/she was told. That anger is really filling your mind. In order to get away from the situation, you rightly give yourself time out and go for a walk. During that walk, angry thoughts are being piled on top of other angry thoughts. It doesn't just apply to anger. It applies to jealousy, greed, obsessions, self-esteem issues and negative outlook. Your mind is filled with all of these negative things. In fact you can even include people whose minds are filled with depression. The walk away from home was to calm you down. Instead of that, you continued to allow bad thoughts to go through your head for whatever reason. In the distance but within your reach, you see a child step off the curb toward the path of an oncoming car. In that split second, what you did was drop all the negativity and goes rescue the child. Your mind didn't need to argue about it. It happened because the need arose.

Thus, from this, you can see that the mind can change direction at any time it needs to. You don't have to hold negative things inside of your mind because they help no one, least of all you. For the time being, you are angry, depressed or whatever else is negative and you're not sure how to get out of that funk. Drop the thought. It's as simple as that; replace it with something more positive.

Before you start trying to do that, you need to learn relaxation as this helps to liberate your mind. Lie down in a room where the light is subdued, where there is no noise and no likelihood of interruption. Make sure that your clothing is comfortable and that your head is supported. This helps your body to breathe without strain. Close your eyes and concentrate on your toes. Tense them – feel them tense – and then relax them so that you feel them becoming heavier. Work your way up your body, actually using your mind to picture that part of your body, to feel it tense and then feel it relax. You work through all the body parts right up to the top of your head. While you are doing this, breathe through the nose and out through the mouth.

At the end of your relaxation stage, get up very slowly and don't rush back into your life. Your mind needs the adjustment to be reasonable.

Positive reinforcement exercises for the mind

If you are on a low par and think yourself unworthy, chances are that your thoughts are all negative. Negative thoughts attract other negative thoughts. Instead of letting this happen you need to positively exercise your mind. Reinforcement exercises for mind stimulation are those that you enjoy and can include the following:

- Doing quizzes like word search
- Crossword puzzles
- Playing Luminosity exercises on the iPad
- Reading the newspaper
- Writing a poem or a letter

These exercises are for the logical part of the brain and are making you think of something while you actually perform some mental exercise. You can't, for example, try to do a crossword puzzle if you keep on thinking bad thoughts. You actually need a measure of concentration. Thus, the crossword clues take precedence over bad thoughts.

Positive reinforcement exercises for your creative side

In a very similar way, the creative side of the brain needs exercise too. Creation that comes from your mind is really good positive reinforcement. It makes you feel good about yourself and that's just what the mind needs. Too much feeling good about yourself and you become vain or bigheaded, but just the right mix can make you feel joyful. If you can think of the following possibilities, these are all useful for exercising the creative side of your brain:

- Drawing a picture
- Making greetings cards
- Putting together a family album
- Making artistic cup cakes
- Learning origami
- Knitting, crochet and needle crafts

There are a whole host of creative things that you can do

within the course of a day, from stitching a button onto a shirt to creating something new from something old. Try your hand at upcycling. It costs nothing and its great fun.

The idea of these exercises for the mind is to take you away from your negativity. When you balance positivity and negativity in equal doses, they are more manageable. When you put negative thoughts out of your mind entirely, you strengthen your own resolve and your mind is much stronger and able to see you through bad patches.

Practice self-control

If you can't give up smoking, tell yourself you can't have one for the next couple of hours and let you, yourself, be in charge of your addiction. If you can't stop eating things that are contributing to your health problems, again limit yourself as to when you can have a treat. ==Make yourself deserve it==. If your mind tells you that you don't like drinking water, you won't drink it. Discipline yourself to drink water by perhaps adding a flavor that makes it more palatable and feel very positive about your achievement. Whether you like it or not, most of your muscular pain is probably something you can handle by simply drinking water. You are not a child. You are a grown up person and if you want to carry on with the agony of dehydration that doctors are too polite to tell you about, then avoiding this liaison between the mind and the body is poison.

[margin note: muscle pain due to dehydration!]
[margin note: What? police? Stupid!]

Self-control means knowing your body and understanding what it is asking for. For example, when I am tired, I sleep. When I am hungry I eat, but the body is much more specific than that if you tap into the energies that tell you what kind of foods your body craves. I tend to crave for green vegetables and found that I actually have a built in iron deficiency and that my body asking for green vegetables is trying to get over the deficiency. Self-control dictates answering to your body when it asks you to do something or to stop doing something. If you do too much physical work, all the pains that you experience are telling you to stop or to change position. Listen to them, as they are there to guide you. My partner does a lot of repetitive carpentry work and found that working repeatedly using the same motions over and over was painful. By adjusting the position, rather than battling on regardless, my partner was able to work for longer and not suffer the pain that had been endured before.

Learning all about your mind

Watch how your body works in conjunction with your mind. You tell yourself you want to eat a cup cake. If there is one around, chances are that you will eat it. Your mind tells you that your pain levels are unacceptable. Your response could be to take a pill in order to feel better, or it could be to find out why your body is feeling so terrible and change whatever it is that's causing it. The thoughts start in the mind. The action is up to you but when you begin to experience giving yourself the right answers; life becomes much easier and less painful to live.

You have one life. If you choose to blame everyone else for all of your troubles, you never fix the troubles. Life's too short for making this kind of decision that someone else or something else is to blame. Take responsibility and you begin to feel so much better because we all know what ails us and what our minds are rejecting. It's time to listen to common sense as it sends you a message, rather than listening to your cravings. Your mind and your cravings are two different things; your mind can use logical reasoning while your cravings use excuses for self-indulgence.

Observing the general rules of good health

Common sense tells us from a very young age that in order to feel great, we need a balanced diet, sleep and exercise in doses that are healthy. As we get older we skew the rules in our favor. Do you really think that eating bagel after bagel you are going to feel good? Imagine all that stodge inside you. It will slow down your metabolism and make you feel sluggish. Is the five-minute thrill of eating it worth that risk? The problem is that we don't want to be told what to do. People feel that their life is their responsibility and that since stories on the news and in the newspapers give varying ideas about the value of different foods, a human can ignore it all and do whatever they please.

Unfortunately, we can't. It's as simple as that. You need a set amount of sleep per night to help your body to heal itself from within and to help solve all the mental dilemmas that you face. You need water to stop dehydration. You need food and need to vary what you eat into the different food groups and most of all, you need to get up out of your armchair and stretch your legs doing gentle exercise that helps you to keep your body in good working order.

Chapter 3 – Listening To Your Body

The body needs good food, plenty of water, exercise and sleep. We have already stated this, but I am stating it again for a purpose. You need that information to sink in. What you may not know is that the hours of sleep allow certain biological and biochemical actions within your body to happen. What these do is to fix things that are wrong. Sleep is a time of healing. It's not just a time to stay awake with your thoughts. If you can't sleep, chances are that your mind is too busy. Try slowing down toward bedtime. Don't watch TV that's hyper active. Try to make your bedroom as inviting as possible and your bedclothes warm enough to give you the comfort your body needs. Try eating less before bedtime as this may be making your digestion work overtime while you try to get off to sleep.

An answer to "I can't sleep, my mind is too active"
When your body is tired and your mind is active, use the mind's active nature to your benefit. In olden days people used to count sheep. That doesn't work very well because it's not a very satisfactory activity to keep your mind off all of

those thoughts. Instead, you need to concentrate on something that does. Imagine driving. Imagine getting into the car and go through all of the actions of driving along a very familiar road.

See your hand change the gear, feel your feet using the accelerator and the brake pedal when needed. See the scenery. Concentrate fully on an activity such as driving because it's all encompassing and doesn't allow other thoughts to get in the way. When I first practiced this, I drove for quite a while but as I improved, I found I was only driving a couple of blocks before I was sound asleep.

Meditation and the help it gives the body

Your subconscious kicks in during the night and is allowed to come out to play. It needs that but you can actually reach your subconscious while you are awake if you learn about different methods of meditation. These don't have to be pie in the sky trendy things to do. Meditation goes back centuries and has been used to help people center themselves so that they create a balance between the mind and the body.

Simple meditation methods that work for busy minds are mindfulness meditation and focused meditation. Mindful meditation means that you make yourself consciously aware of all the activities that you do in your life. For example, when you eat – you chew your food thoroughly and enjoy all the textures and tastes. When you breathe, you feel the air entering your body and feel it when you exhale. You are aware of the moment in which you currently are and don't let past thoughts clutter your brain or worries about tomorrow because it may never happen. You can close your eyes and simply enjoy being you. That brings the subconscious out to play more often and makes you very happy inside.

In focused meditation, you sit in a calm spot and you think of something that's made you very happy indeed. This could be a scene that you can concentrate on that reminds you of the best happiness you ever experienced. Close your eyes, picture it, be there and enjoy the moment thoroughly without letting your mind wander to other things.

Listening to your bodily needs

If a man breaks his leg, he doesn't automatically hop because the other leg is stronger. The pain comes first and the inability to cope with the situation. It's very similar with bodily needs. When you are hungry, ask yourself whether you really are or whether your body is letting your cravings tell you that you are hungry. Change snacks for healthier alternatives. When your body has cramps, is it because something is seriously wrong? The cramps may just be telling you that you lack magnesium or that you haven't been drinking your quota of water.

When you have a headache, don't automatically grab the pills. See why you have a headache. Did you watch too much TV too loud? Did you spend too much time at the computer? There are ways to alter things that may not need pills. For example, changing the resolution on the TV may make the screen more relaxing to watch. The computer color can be toned down to attempt to stop you from having headaches. Let your mind work on your bodily problems and often the solution comes from inside you, rather than external remedy.

Your body may be stiff. Perhaps you don't use your arms and your legs sufficiently. When you get up, they stiffen because they haven't had any exercise. You don't have to become a marathon runner overnight, but how about a nice walk in the park. Get yourself a puppy and you give yourself a reason to walk in the park and a reason to actually feel good about sharing your home. Your mind has solutions. You just need to start listening to them. The healing that takes place in the body and the mind begins with listening.

Your mind is probably filled to brimming with all kinds of things and you need to let some of these go. If you find yourself thinking in a negative manner about anything, consciously switch course and replace a negative with a positive. You may find that a bit unnatural at first but if you look around you at the people that you know, you will find that those who are happiest are those who don't spread negativity. They are empathetic – that means they can put themselves into someone else's shoes – and understand people a lot better than those who simply criticize. It's actually mind opening to realize the problems that others have because it tends to make you a happier person when you are able to offer help, without expecting any reward from it.

Listening to your body includes the following:

- Knowing where aches and pains are coming from
- Knowing what is worrying you and being able to drop worry
- Knowing when your physical pain is caused by mental anguish
- Knowing when mental anguish is being caused by physical pain.

The last two items on that list look the same but they are totally different. Often if you know what the physical cause of something is, it doesn't worry you as much as it did when you were not sure of where the pain was coming from. Often people visit doctors more for reassurance than anything else and may well be given placebos or merely reassurance and that's enough to make the pain go away. If the pain comes from mental anguish, I have a chapter later in the book that will help you to overcome this, so that your pain will consequently lessen and become more manageable. The point is that listening to your body is an absolute essential if you want to change your life.

Chapter 4 - Learning Not To Be A Martyr

People who act the martyr are usually very unhappy people. I remember someone from my past who was this way inclined and would do things for other people. She did that, not because she was empathetic, but because she was always seeking reward. She loved telling people of all the good that she had done, but she also had a very bad habit of reminding them of how much she had sacrificed in order to do something for them. Consequently, she was never satisfied and always unhappy. If you find that you have been prepared to do things for people but that you expected something in exchange, you need to change your approach. You can't expect anything. It's not your place to. If you choose to give and give of your own free will, give with a good heart, expecting absolutely nothing in return and holding no strings over those you give to.

There's a lot of positivity to be learned from this gesture. If you are doing things for someone simply to make yourself a spectacle, then stop. It isn't helping you and it certainly is not helping anyone long term because your level of expectation is wrongly placed. Try doing something today. It's an experiment to show you what it's like to give and to expect nothing in return. If you know an old lady in your area that doesn't have many visitors bake a cake or go offer to fix a fence panel or a rotten step at the front of their house. Do it with all of your love and give that elderly person something for nothing. The gratitude that you get shouldn't be taken for granted because the lesson you are learning is not about giving and taking. <u>It's not about gratitude and favors. It's not even about expectation. It's about feeling good within yourself that you were able to help someone and did. That's all the reward that you need</u>. Do this often instead of thinking in a negative way. Help someone cross a busy road. Hold an umbrella over someone to stop him or her from getting wet. Give without expecting any kind of return and your whole life changes for the better. You may not notice it straight away, but you will feel like your life has some kind of purpose. People who expect gratitude and then get none set themselves up for disappointment and bitterness and that's not very good for their mental state at all. It can lead to depression, resentment, unhelpfulness and even to using statements like these, which are really unhealthy:

It's the least you can do for me. You owe me.

This is a nonsense statement. <u>No one owes you anything</u>. Every human being has to live their own life without trying to tie people up in knots by blackmail. If you find yourself telling someone that they owe you a debt of some kind, then you make yourself unhappy. I once gave a total stranger $100 because his needs were more than mine. At no time was I expecting to get this back although he surprised me. When he had set himself up and had managed to dig himself out of the hole in which his life was buried, he actually knocked at the door of my home and gave it back. It wasn't hard for him to find me, since I had found this troubled soul at the end of my driveway, out in the road.

Don't be a martyr to your illness

People are very ready to spread the misery of their illness and what they may be doing is creating negativity. Yes, it's okay to complain a little if you hurt, but there are those who actually use their illness as a means to gain sympathy. It's usually meaningless if you have to play this game and it's a very negative game to play. People begrudge helping you because they feel you are pulling them down with you. It's time for a wake-up call. Every human being goes through illness at some stage, whether it's physical illness or the strain of mental illness. Don't make yours more important than everyone else's.

You need to examine your illness, to find out why it's happening and do something positive to make it better. Of course, with mental anguish you can't just make it go away without work, which is outlined in the next chapter, but physical illness happens for a reason. If you cough a lot and want sympathy from people for your constant state of bronchitis, cut down on your smoking! I have known people who smoke two packs a day and actually expect me to be sympathetic toward their illness. Sympathy only goes so far.

You know what's better than being a martyr to your illness and is much more positive? Spreading news that is very positive is always good and always welcomed by people. It makes them happier and it makes you happier. When you discover how to make your physical pains better, share it with someone who can benefit from it. There was a physical fitness teacher in a village I lived in and he was the most positive person I have ever met. His life was happy and he taught physical fitness because he had once been in a car crash and had discovered how to recover from his injuries quickly with exercise. Seeing others suffer, he worked hand in hand with a physiotherapist and found that he could help others become more mobile. Instead of using the illness to become a martyr, he used it to positive benefit to help others to feel that positivity and that's a wonderful thing.

You may have seen people who are nearing the end of their lives with serious illnesses starting to raise funds or raise awareness for others with that illness. You see advertisements on the television. These are people who have no hope of a long life expectancy and yet they are not spreading negativity. Instead they are making the last days of their lives filled to brimming with positivity and are setting a wonderful example that healthy people really should benefit from. They say that when you are being treated for cancer and illnesses of this magnitude, positive attitude goes a long way toward healing. McMillan Nurses in the United Kingdom and Hospice Nurses in other countries all over the world work with people who are dying but the one thing that they all say is that positive people make their illness much more bearable because they are not prepared to lie down and die in pain. That's got to teach you something about what the body needs.

If you choose, instead, to live your illness, you don't get cured. There was an allergy group that I once visited as part of my work. Every week, people who were being treated for allergies were encouraged to get together to discuss their ailments. I thought at first that this was quite a positive way of dealing with rare allergies because people who suffer from them are often very alone.

However, what I found was that the kinds of people who attended was those looking for more symptoms and checking out their allergies against others and it became almost a competition between patients to develop new allergies. These people were living their illnesses. If you want to live your illness, you will never feel healed. You will never feel the happiness that comes with healing. If that sounds anything like you, then it's time to move forward and find a way where your attitude toward illness is changed and becomes much more positive, using the methods detailed in the next chapter.

I am a very happy person and the healing that I have discovered in my life is amazing. I wanted this book to convey that sense of healing because it puts life back into perspective and it helps you to go through all the hurdles that life puts in front of you easily, knowing that each bad moment will pass and that it will be filled with more happy moments. Healing your life means looking deeply into who you are and cutting out all the negativity that you spread by accepting defeat and becoming a martyr to it. You do no one any favors at all treating illness in this way and the next chapter shows you how to move on from physical and mental pain to a place where your life offers much more and allows you more freedom to be creative and happy.

Section 2: Conventional Methods of healing

Chapter 5 – Exercises In Mindfulness

Mindfulness is an awareness that people don't always possess. Of course people are conscious from the moment they wake up in the morning but how they see life may differ from those who are not just conscious, but mindful. In a class, I was taught about mindfulness and at first found it a little restricting, but it was only me that was restricting my own progress, rather than anyone else.

Finding a place of grounding

What this means is finding a place on this Earth where you really are at peace with life. My place is at the top of a hill, which has a small church on it. It's no longer used, but at this height above the ground below, the view that I get is stunning. Why do you need a place like this? You need to find somewhere that brings out awe in you. It's a place where everything worldly is put aside. You don't take your pains there. You don't have room in your mind for negative thoughts and you surround yourself by the beauty of the place. People often visit the Northern Lights for this reason but your chosen place doesn't have to be that elaborate. It can be a local park that you enjoy or a hill above your city. It can be a waterfall or a beach at sunset. The point is that it must be special to you and have enough beauty that it puts everything else into perspective.

Standing on the top of the hill that I chose, for example, I could see all the colors of the hills in their evening dress, against a sky of red and the most important thing is that whatever place you find should make you feel small and insignificant in comparison. I discovered this when I visited this special place and I wasn't expecting it. Up until that moment, I had been living my illness and had felt quite sorry for myself. I had also had a lot of negative thoughts and didn't have many friends because of it. Here I was, on top of a hill and against what I saw, I was like a small pebble on a beach. I felt somehow close to God and even if you are a non-believer, you get this sense of spirituality that you can't explain in any other way than being something greater than you. It then occurred to me that each of the elements that were filling my mind with awe were small things which made up into that whole scene; a tree in the distance, a red sun, a bright orange cloud, a field of heather, etc. I was one of these small things, so I was just as essential to life as anything else that I was looking at.

When you find your place of grounding, you can use mindfulness to make you very aware of the moment that you are in, rather than the future or the past. Mindfulness dismisses past and dismisses future because one has gone and the other has not yet arrived. The only point in time that you have in this instance of time is NOW. Thus, you need to feel good about it or it's wasted. So, how do you achieve this if you feel so bad about your life? The trick is to learn to breathe, to learn to meditate and in doing so, learn to harmonize the body mind connection that helps pain to become less.

Meditation exercises

These help in all kinds of circumstances and you can do mindful meditation at any time in your life when you want to step away from any kind of pain, whether physical or mental pain. You just need a peaceful place to experience it. This can be a quiet park, your bedroom or somewhere where there is relatively little distraction. People even use this form of meditation to energize themselves and ready for business meetings because it clears out all the cobwebs within the brain, helps makes you feel better and see life much more clearly.

Sit in a position where you back is nice and straight because this helps energy to flow correctly. If you want to walk, you can choose this option as well, but you can only do this once you have learned the process sitting down and when you have mastered breathing in the way I am about to suggest. For this initial practice and until you are better at it, close your eyes. This stops distractions. Make sure that you are comfortably attired because if you have a tight waistband, your attention will keep drifting off to that tightness and that's not where you will find any calmness.

Breathe in through the nose and concentrate only on that breath going into your lungs. Feel it enter your body and then hold it for a moment before breathing out from the lower part of your abdomen. Every time you breathe out, count one. The only thing that you should think about is your breathing and the counting as you go from one up to ten. If you start thinking about something else, start again at one and when you reach ten, start again at one.

When you first start to do this exercise give yourself about quarter of an hour. That means that you can practice it at lunchtime or in a convenient moment in your day. Usually mornings are not the best time because your energy levels are at their highest, so you need them for performing whatever tasks you have to do. Thus, when the tasks are finished or when you have a break, this routine is good for your health and your mental wellbeing.

You can increase the time, as you get better at dismissing thoughts from your mind. You can also do it with your eyes open, if you are able to avoid being distracted by what you see. You can even focus on a given point and not move your eyes from it. People use all kinds of things like a Buddha statue or a flower in the garden or even a postcard on a door to give the eyes a focal point so that they are not looking everywhere and losing the whole point of meditation. The idea is to give yourself a specific target for your thoughts and your senses and this is your breathing. Thus all distractions take away from the benefits of meditation.

I find that useful even today when my life is healed already and I am very happy in my life. You can still get times when you run out of energy. You can still get times when the weather gets you down or when your thought processes are not as positive as you would like them to be. If you take time to observe people in a busy street café, you will see that there are those who are happy to be still and silent while others insist in filling their heads with noise and movement. The problem today is that we fill up minds to overflow with problems that are not very important. Then, when physical pain is added to the equation, we get to a point where we cannot cope any more. Thus, meditation brings you back to neutral ground. There are no kids screaming. There is no boss shouting at you for work you should have done yesterday. In that moment of meditation, there is nothing except breathing.

Mindful meditation in your lifestyle

It's quite likely that you go through life without noticing things. Often you don't look at the flowers in the gardens on the way to work. You don't look at the color of the sky or the beauty of everything that surrounds you in life. Mindfulness encourages you to make more of what's there. When you eat, for example, don't rush your meal in order to get back to work. Take your time. Savor the food, enjoy the different textures and tastes and you will not only feel great after eating, but you will begin to discover that eating at this pace gives you real taste to cherish and a digestive system that is eternally grateful that you didn't eat your food quickly.

Mindfulness means just being aware of the moment that you are in. It's no more complex than that. Don't carry the emotional baggage from yesterday. It's your choice to drop it. It's only unresolved while you still let it into your life. Use other stimuli to help you to avoid negative thoughts of what's happened in your life. None of that matters any more really. It's gone. Now is the moment and if you fill each moment with something worthwhile like living in it, rather than drifting from past negative events to future worry, you actually find that you are suddenly healed. Emotionally, you are able to offer much more to the people you know and those that you meet and physically, you don't hide who you are behind an illness or a pain of some sort. You can live a life which is much more enjoyable.

People use affirmations sometimes to feel better about things in their lives. I personally find these a little restrictive. Instead of wishing your life away wanting to be something that you are not, it's going to happen quicker if you use mindfulness because you actually get to enjoy being who you are and people who do that attract other positive people who make life a wonderful place to be.

Does your pain go away?

To a certain extent it does because what changes is the way that you see it. People who are balanced and happy see pain as a small inconvenience and are stronger in their resistance to pain and less likely to suffer it as a consequence of negative thinking. People who don't use positive thought and mindfulness tend to hide behind pain. They use it as an excuse for not doing something, or as an excuse for not being as functional as they should be. They tell you that they can't exercise because of their illness whereas someone who is mindful will take joy in exercise even if that's only a walk in the park with the dog.

Pain is actually a signal from a part of the body to the brain but its how your mind perceives it and what it does with it once it happens that makes all the difference in the pain levels.

Does it help mental anguish?

Yes, there is a definite connection between practicing mindfulness and positivity. The reason for this is that mindful people don't tend to look backwards because that's not what mindfulness is about. It's always about now. Thus, if your worries come from the past, they are not permitted to affect who you are now. Problems are a bit like that. When they arise, they become as large or as small a problem as you perceive them to be. You need to decide about the criteria upon which you accept problems. Look at the different categories below and you will see that these are clear-cut.

- Problems you can do something about
- Problems you can't do something about
- Problems that have no significance in the now

The ones that you can do something about need tending to especially if they happen now. If these are left not dealt with, they may grow into bigger problems. Thus, the first priority of any day is to get those out of the way first. I can stop the mosquito bites from last night from hurting. Thus I place a cream on them. I can stop my waistband from hurting. Thus, I change the outfit. I can stop myself from being negative in this moment in time – thus I make a conscious effort to be more agreeable.

Problems that you can't do anything about are those that you need to drop. For example, if your loved one chose to leave you – yes it hurts – but no amount of negative thought will bring your true love back again. You can't be in control of someone else's thoughts. People tend to use their weakness and their sadness to try and guilt a partner into coming back but the fact that the partner left in the first place means that somewhere along the line, the relationship died. You can't change that and negative thoughts about it won't help you to develop as a person. Perhaps you even changed yourself to such an extent that you became negative and bitter. That is something you can do something about and perhaps when you do, your partner may change their view. There are no guarantees. What you need to be aware of is that the only things that you are in control of are those things that you can change. Walk away from those that you can't.

Problems that have no significance in the now are those that you can do nothing about. You know they need to be resolved one day but its other people that need to resolve them. These are problems you need to put aside. If they don't matter in the now, forget them because you can't do anything to make them change. The "what ifs" and the "If only" attitudes in life are pointless and waste so much mental energy that they serve no purpose to your wellbeing.

Instead of thinking about the past or worrying about the future, keep yourself grounded for a whole week in the present and you will discover that it really helps heal the way that you think and the way that you see things like pain, illness, thought processes and how it strengthens you so that when something does happen to your health, you don't respond to it in such a negative way and it doesn't become such a huge problem. The happiness that you will achieve through this method of meditation is amazing and you will start to see the best side of life. This, in turn, will help you to attract those people who are positive and that also improves your life and changes it considerably.

Chapter 6 – Making Your Life Happy

Your life being happy depends on several things. You need sufficient of all of these elements to make your life a worthwhile place to be:

- Friendships
- Celebrations
- Victories
- Self-confidence
- Belief in self
- Reasonable health

All of these contribute toward the way your mind and your body reacts to life. For example, someone with no friendships may feel despondent and unhappy because they need that warmth that they lack. In consequence, lonely people can actually begin to believe that they don't have the same right to happiness as others and can fall into illness more easily than those who have happy relationships with others.

The celebrations of life don't have to be vast ones. These are the reasons to feel happy and to share that happiness. When you pass your exams, when you give birth to your first baby, all of these kinds of events reinforce your purpose in life and are very positive; happy events that help contribute to feeling well in mind and body.

Finding your purpose in life

If you are unhappy, try going to a place that inspires you. Perhaps from the top of a hill confronted by nature, you can find some of the answers that you have been searching for. There's an inner calm and peace when you are surrounded by nature and are awe struck by its vastness. It puts things into perspective and makes you experience how small you are in comparison to everything else. How does this help? It helps you because people who feel humbled are more likely to enjoy their lives and appreciate everything around them. They are less likely to take things for granted and can use a spiritual retreat such as this to get back to their roots, exercising the body getting there and exercising the mind when viewing the spectacle chosen as awe inspiring.

When you feel this oneness with the world, you also feel very healthy inside. You may have ill health but you still feel whole. A cancer patient who knew that she only had a few months to live startled me once. She was so happy in herself and able to accept her fate with grace, but when I asked her why, it transpired that she had found that comfortable space between mind and body that wasn't going to make her tread the negative path for the time that she had left. She embraced life regardless of her ailment. She found her place in life and when she did that, she didn't suffer all of the downtime that many patients in her place would have suffered. Her body mind connection was perfectly honed to happiness.

Her example actually made me think because delving deeper,

she told me how she had been able to overcome all the negativity and replace it with positive thought. She was a believer in herself and in her God, and had told herself that you cannot change fate. You cannot cheat it and no amount of worrying about it is likely to change the outcome. Instead of her allotted couple of months, she actually went on to live a much longer time and enjoyed it all because she gave herself purpose. What human beings often mistake is the need for purpose. Lazy people stay in bed because they have nothing to get up for. She introduced something into her life that was worthwhile, and people who do this have a very positive mind-body liaison that helps them. By being available to other cancer patients, she improved their lot and gave herself incentive to get up the next day, regardless of how her body was feeling.

My purpose was found in writing. Why? There are a whole host of reasons but the enjoyment of writing and the experience of sharing was something my life afforded me time for. Again, you need to find a purpose, no matter how mundane that purpose may appear. It's not about show. It's about knowing in your heart and mind that you did something to make a difference. Find your purpose. Find your aim and you begin to find your place in life. This helps to sustain you and helps you to make the right decisions about caring for your body and feeding your mind.

The mind-body connection

It doesn't take a physically strong person to be mentally powerful. It doesn't take a brainchild to be physically fit. Thus, one may assume that the two are not linked. That assumption would be incorrect. The mind and body interconnect in ways you can only imagine. If you feed your mind positivity, this helps you to heal your body. If you feed your body exercise, food and drink, this helps your body to sustain your ability to think in a positive manner. Thus, both are intrinsically interlinked. To heal your body, you must therefore, heal your mind and vice versa.

Dealing with chronic pain is something that is difficult for everyone. It's not fun waking up day after day with the same pain but you can change things by learning about your illness and doing everything that you can to help escape it. For example, people who have muscle problems can avoid a lot of the pain that they experience by understanding nutritional needs and which foods to avoid helping the problem. More water is always a good starting point. Then people argue that they drink water in tea and coffee but as a physiotherapist explained to me, coffee and tea are different to water, even though they are made with it. If you drink one cup of coffee, you actually urinate between 2-3 cups. That effectively means that you are dehydrating your body and that water is being expelled from your body that is not being replaced.

People who are chronically obese need also to understand about what they can do to help their own situation. There is always something you can do but you need to have a greater understanding and only you can glean that from knowing what you eat, how much activity you have in the course of a day, and what you can do to fix the problem of excess calories without resorting to having to count them all. Things that people don't understand about nutrition are things like replacing sugar with sweeteners. With natural sugar giving you a high for longer, when you use sweeteners, you crave more sugar because the sweetener's ability to give you that sugar high is relatively short. Similarly, those that eat too much fruit may not be conscious of the fact that excessive fruit also adds too much sugar to the system.

I looked into a lot of the pains that I experienced and many of them were self-inflicted although I hadn't been aware of it. When you investigate, it's actually quite easy to make your life a better place to be. If you don't like walking, but know you have to, why not get a dog? Often people who are obese suffer from self-esteem problems, but the positivity of having a pet means that they are more likely to walk if not for themselves, for their well-loved pet. One pain I experienced that did make life hell was pain in the wrist. I investigated this and watched out for triggers and my iPad was the cause. By using a cushion to place the iPad on, I no longer had to strain my wrist every time I wanted to spend any length of time on the iPad.

Making your life a happier place

If you use mindfulness, it will make you more aware of things that you do that make you unhappy. It will also give your mind a rest from time to time, which is needed by everyone. Remember the importance of regular sleep because this also helps you to be a happier person. When studies were done on people's wellbeing, it wasn't surprising that those who had a good night's sleep were more productive and found life easier than those who spent too little time sleeping. Since we already know that the body heals itself during sleep and that the subconscious deals with problems while you are asleep, if you deprive yourself of sleep, you deprive yourself of these benefits.

What I found when I woke up one morning and didn't hurt any more was that I had adopted a new style to my life. I had a routine that was healthy. I slept the right amount of time, ate regular meals that were not excessive and occasionally treated myself. None of it included denying me anything. Often people diet because they are unhappy about their weight and then they become unhappy because they feel that their restrictive diet deprives them. It's one whole vicious circle. I found that changing my food to good food that was enjoyable instead of calorie packed foods, I started to taste new things and I didn't go hungry at all.

You also need to take a look at the people who make you unhappy. Often people that surround you dictate how happy you are. If you surround yourself with people who are critical or who are negative all of the time, some of that negativity is going to rub off on you.

Of course, friendship is give and take, but you need to help the healing process by deciding which people actually add to your life and which don't and drop the dead wood. If they are really negative people, then they will always find someone else to lay their burden on but it's not helping your health or your happiness to let them spoil your life. People like this thrive on attention and upon using others. They are opportunists and you need to be very strong-minded about taking their opportunity away from your doorstep.

When you mix with people who are positive your life is more positive as a result. That positivity gives you strength to help friends who deserve your strength and those will be the same people who give and take in equal doses and add something to the happiness aspect of your life.

Chapter 7 – Spoiling Yourself

While people are filled with ideas of things that YOU should do, they may not know the things that you like and want to treat yourself to. The problems that occur within the family unit are that people have expectations of you. Young people get married. They work toward getting a home together and then the responsibility of children comes along. There's a lot of sacrifice made along the way but its all part of family life. However, you need to turn that around and tell yourself that you are entitled to time for yourself to do the things that you want to do.

It's sometimes not enough to be Mrs. or mom, or grandma. You want to be you but life doesn't let you. Make yourself a bucket list of the things that you want to do. Be sure that you let everyone know what your bucket list is and encourage those around you to make theirs as well.

That way, you open up a dialog so that when you do come to fulfill an item on your bucket list, it won't come as a complete shock to people and they will be pleased that you are fulfilling a dream. We often put dreams on the back shelf in favor of reality and that's a sad state of affairs because it can lead to resentment later in life, resentment that you never got to do all of those things that you once dreamed that you would.

How it feels when you fulfill a dream

Your dreams may cost a little bit of money, but if you have a definite vision of what they are, you can work toward achieving them and this really gives you a real high in life. One of the things that I wanted to do was jump from an aircraft.

You may think this isn't that good at helping the course of healing but that depends how you do it and the instruction that you have. Of course, when you do it with the right teacher, it's a wonderfully powerful feeling and the adrenaline kick that you get from that ambition can really give you a sense of achievement.

I haven't yet fulfilled my main bucket list item, which is to sit underneath the Northern Lights, but I am nearer to it now than I ever have been. Having sorted out all my health problems and having become much happier about who I am, I decided that my bucket list items were not a lot to ask of life. The Northern Lights ambition was something that I looked into and was cheaper than I imagined. What it means is putting aside a little money when I can and when I have enough, I can do it.

We put restrictions on ourselves by not really knowing what's involved in our dreams. For example, for 10 years I have been talking about the Northern Lights and yet never thought it was actually possible within my lifetime because I didn't know enough about it. If you want to chase your dreams and make your life really happy and fulfilled, at least take on the responsibility of finding out how to do that thing that you have in your mind. Find out what it costs and never put it off as something you can never have for yourself. By putting away a little here and there, you can work toward something when you know what that something is.

In everyday life

It's great to treat yourself occasionally and remember that you are important. Your body is important as well and if you want to give it a great treat, then why not do that? Treats take all shapes and formats and buying a bubble bath may even be enough to make you feel special. You deserve it.

Being greedy isn't a very positive way to be, but learning that you are entitled to treat yourself occasionally boosts the way that you feel. I used to set myself goals and these always help in health problems and in personal emotional problems. For example, I decided that when I managed to increase my meditation time, I deserved a treat and it wasn't even anything expensive. It was some luxury tea that I had always loved but never bought for myself.

On another occasion, I treated myself to a new drawing book and some fresh watercolors because I was worth it. I had been working with student paints for a long time and at the beginning, these were just right for my level of experience. However, if you get better at something why not use better materials. The treat is worth it. Similarly, I was a little scared of starting to play the guitar. I didn't want a great deal of expense on my first guitar because I was afraid that I might never learn to play it.

After two years on a budget guitar, I had earned the right to have a better guitar. My playing justified it and the treat really boosted my feeling of happiness. After another year of lessons, I even treated myself to the amplifier to go with it.

These may sound like expensive treats but treats don't have to be expensive. They can be of little rewards you give to yourself for your great achievements. Treating yourself to a glass of wine isn't that indulgent, though if you don't generally drink wine, then it can seem rather special. Your treats are just feel good things. An occasional cupcake can make you feel like a million dollars provided that you have merited it and aren't adding to health problems. Think of it as an occasional thing rather than an everyday thing because that's the great thing about treating yourself. If it were too often, it wouldn't be a treat.

To help your looks

Treats to help your looks don't have to be expensive either. Perhaps, if you are a man, you may want to treat yourself to a beard trimmer or a manicure set or even a crisp new shirt or a sports shirt. Women are a little more complex in their beauty needs but there's nothing quite as nice as feeling that skin after a facial wax. If you can't afford to go out to a salon, microwave-peeling wax makes it easy for you to do it yourself.

Often your looks get you down as well as your health. A makeover can help boost your confidence and clearing out the closet can be so rewarding. You may even find that you can recycle some of the clothing that hasn't seen the light of day for years. When you heal yourself, you feel you want to show the world how good you feel and changing your style can do this. Instead of feeling dowdy, try something new and different. It doesn't have to cost a lot of money.

A new color to your hair can make you feel ten years younger. Streaks can make you feel upbeat and modern.

Maybe a home hair dye will be all that you need or all that you can afford but there are such good quality dyes are relatively inexpensive and can give you a real boost morally because healing yourself and changing your life take you through very positive experiences and these experiences are well worth the trouble.

<u>Whatever it takes to make you happy, go for it</u>. It may be swimming at the local pool, attending yoga with friends or just going out once a week to somewhere you have never been whether on foot or in the car. Life is filled to brimming with new experiences and when you grab the opportunity you find that these open doors to happiness you never thought you may be capable of experiencing.

Chapter 8 – Embracing Positive Creativity

Your brain has two sides. One is used for logical things and the other is used for creative activity. Often people don't use the creative side as much as they should. You may have noticed that people around you are gifted with different crafts and its great fun to exercise this side of the brain and also helps you when you want to get beyond physical illness. I love crafts and have tried all kinds and there is always something that you can do even if you consider yourself to be less than gifted. For example, making candles can be beneficial from two viewpoints – because you can incorporate aromatherapy essential oils, which give you a really good feeling inside when they are lit and placed in the bedroom or in the bathroom. Small votive candles are cheap to make but make great gifts for people when placed in a really nice glass container.

Why is creativity good for the brain?

It makes you feel like you have achieved something. There's nothing quite as nice as seeing a finished sweater, a finished painting, embroidery, wood carving or something of that nature that you know that you made with your own ideas and your own two hands. In many situations in hospitals where people are ill long term, they have classes where patients can go to do different crafts and these can easily be incorporated into your life. It may be worthwhile doing some searches online for crafts that you may never have heard of such as "Entangle" which is a form of art to help people to feel more relaxed and it works great for stress. This is where you draw like you might have done while on the telephone, but your doodles are much more organized. People of all ages are enjoying this. Pottery with air-drying clay is another thing you can play with although one of the most positive things to come out of this commercialized world is upcycling, where you take an old item, which is no longer in use, and make it into something useful.

Creativity is good for the brain because it fills you with positivity. In a way, as well, when you are concentrating on something like crafts, you are banishing all those negative thoughts and are able to ground yourself in much the same way as you do when you meditate. Stand in front of a sketchpad and draw your local village church, or start pressing flowers. Even a scrapbook of family pictures and memorabilia can be a creative outlet that allows you that freedom of expression that life often denies the individual because of the constraints of their lives.

Painting and Writing as good choices

These two choices are particularly good for people who are seeking healing. These allow self-expression but they allow more than that. The words of a poem may be positively healing. Poetry is a way to put words and thoughts into something more constructive than keeping them locked inside where they can do harm to your mental state. If you are angry, get the words out into a poem and illustrate it, even if you're not talented at drawing. Add decoupage, which is cut out images stuck to a page to make the poem look really presentable. If you practice poetry for therapy purposes, you can actually get good at it and start to use it for really positive purposes like greetings cards and sharing with friends and family.

Painting is also a very expressive art. Angry at life? Don't ever let anger fester inside you. Splash it onto the canvas in as bright a red as you want to because all of this helps you to get negative thoughts out of your system. You may even find you have a talent for it but <u>the positivity you gain from art and writing is amazing.</u>

A healing exercise

I remember an exercise that I used to do when I wasn't happy. First thing in the morning, I would sit at a computer screen and I would devote the time it took me to drink my morning coffee opening up a Word document and letting my fingers type. There was no purpose to this other than being an outlet for whatever thoughts were festering and sometimes I even surprised myself at what came out. It's not guided writing, which is controlled by someone else. It was simply allowing me to spontaneously pour out thoughts onto paper without thinking about them at all. There was no planning. This had to be spontaneous. Others have told me that they did the same thing with writing into a journal and yet others used a writing exercise whenever they felt angry.

They picked up a writing pad, wrote a letter to address their anger and then scrunched it up and threw it away and when they did that, all of the negative anger was gone. That's how temporary negative things such as anger are but you do need to release them. You remember the swear words you said silently to yourself while you festered? Instead of doing that, write it down, screw it up or tear it into tiny pieces and throw it away, but make sure that it's somewhere where no one has a chance to read it!

You need to understand all the things that make a human being feel negative and when you do, you will see that these may be things you let into your life. The list below is by no means exhaustive, but all of these are negative:

- Greed
- Jealousy
- Anger
- Hate
- Resentment

When anyone lets any of these elements into their lives, they also open the door to negativity, which will take away any power from healing processes. Thus, you need to deal with these feelings and banish them from your life. Meditation as shown in another chapter will help you, but also keeping a journal or painting a picture can help get these feelings out of your system. Jealousy is fruitless. You are who you are and you have what you have. You need to accept something essential to wellbeing and that is:

What is and who you are

I used to go through a stage of not liking myself very much and in retrospect I can see where all that negativity came from. I measured myself against others. I wasn't the best looking. I didn't have the best clothes. I felt ashamed sometimes of the passed down clothing that I wore, but when I grew out of that, I realized that being me was actually something unique and I didn't have to pretend to be someone else or dress or act in a way that anyone dictated in magazines and in media. What I did need to do was accepting who I was and embrace the uniqueness of my own approach. I didn't have to conform to wearing jeans and tee shirts because other people did. What I did need was to just enjoy being me. What is and who you are is vital to happiness and acceptance turned a great big corner because when I became happy within myself, and used my creative side, I found that I had more friends, I had more opportunities and enjoyed everything about my life.

An exercise in creativity

The choice is yours. You can either use paper and pen or you can use acrylic paints and pebbles. Choose your weapons. With these elements create something original. It really doesn't matter what it is, but make it something that expresses who you are. These are easy materials to get together and the variety of things that you can do with these simple materials is vast. Write a poem – write a thought and decorate the page. Draw or cut the paper into paper flowers or origami. Make the pebble into a painted creature or make it into a symbol of peace. Whatever you choose to do, keep the object you end up with as a reminder to yourself that this was a turning point for you, one when you were not prepared to be negative anymore and chose to move forward making your life a place of wonder and creation, peace and harmony as well as encouraging good health and happiness.

Chapter 9 – Working Your Way through Mental and Physical Pain

The chances are that you bought this book to find solutions. Your mental struggles may be too much for you, or your physical pain may be getting you down to the extent that you can't function. Throughout the book, we have explained the link between healing the mind and healing the body. In the course of a lifetime, there are times when you may feel that you can't be healed. The lady who was given several months to live could justifiably argue that there was no cure, though she didn't seek one. She came to terms with her illness because she had strength of mind and perfect balance between her mind and body. She accepted the inconvenience of illness but was not prepared to be a victim of it.

Similarly, there are really hard times for people who lose loved ones or who go through divorce or difficult moments that they cannot cope with. The reason mind/body balance is so important is because the mind gives the body more strength when needed and the body that is strong helps to make the suffering of mental dilemma seem more in proportion. Of course, events will happen that are unexpected and which knock you out for six, but if you have built a solid foundation for your life in all of the ways shown within this book, you have prepared yourself and given yourself the strong roots that you need in order to be able to face those times and to triumph over them, rather than letting them pull you down even further. It's important to maximize your happiness so that you can cope through bad times and mindfulness will also help you to get by ~~through~~ these times, one moment at a time.

Imagine the man who has a weak mind filled with negativity and a weak body that ails him because of pains. He may not want to listen to the messages being sent to him about his bodily needs. The suffering smothers the messages and he in turn loses the opportunity to improve his own situation.

However, those who are unhappy can use positive and affirmative action to get the mind back on track as shown in previous chapters. Of course, there are always going to be sad moments in everyone's life, but they don't all spend all of their nights and days lost in the negative land of self-indulgence. People who lose a partner get through the grief stages at different rates of speed. When they do get to the other side, they are able to see the positive side of the time shared with that partner and that makes their lives very worthwhile indeed.

When someone is ill and has a day of remission, that day gives them mental strength and positivity. It can therefore be seen clearly that positive thoughts come from positive body messages. Positive body condition can also help the mental processes of the mind. These are so linked and so simple to tackle. If thoughts are negative, find out why and move on. Do something proactive. Do something to make the negatives into positives because the strength that you gain from doing this is amazing.

These days, there is so much talk about self-love and putting it into those words sometimes puts people off actually liking themselves very much. It sounds a little arrogant to love yourself. It sounds selfish when we are taught to be unselfish from childhood. It goes against the teachings we had as children about always being aware of others. If you can look at it another way, you may be able to see it in better perspective, as I did. I didn't much like the idea of self-love. It sounded twee. However, when I learned to listen to my mind and body and respect its wishes, I achieved the same thing. I began to actually love my life and respect my own beliefs in life as well as enjoying life to the full, regardless of how my body felt. If you take the time to listen to your own needs, it's not selfishness. Its survival and its common sense, but it amounts to the same as self-love.

Your body may not be the shape you want it to be, but once you accept it as being part of who you are, you can listen to messages from your body and heed them. If your body tells you that you have eaten sufficient, don't eat more simply to appear polite. If your body tells you that you don't want another alcoholic drink, but that you'd really like a glass of ice cool water, listen to it. Your body is actually telling you it's dehydrated and needs that water to feel well again.

Healing of your body and your mind becomes a very natural instinct once you hone in on it. Forget the negative thoughts, the jealousy, the greed and the regrets. These won't help either your body or your mind. Learn to understand, forgiving, kind and empathetic and you actually get to like being who you are. That's when happiness starts.

Chapter 10 – Healing Through Meditation

Meditation is one of the best ways to heal your mind and body. This method starts with the mind and slowly moves into improving your body. You will find that you are able to ensure that you spread a sense of calm through your mind and your body. When you meditate, you will find yourself reflecting on your actions. You will also be able to reflect on the consequences of the actions that you would have taken. When you meditate on a regular basis, you will find that you are able to answer many questions of which the following are the most common and important:

1. Do my actions cause stress? Am I causing suffering to myself and to the people around me?
2. Have my actions led to immense stress leading to chronic headaches and anxiety? Have I been unable to function well because of this stress?
3. If I know that they cause unnecessary stress to me, why do I still do it?

4. Since I know that my actions are harming me, can I convert them into a skill?

You have learnt that you can answer the questions that are eating you up on a regular basis! But, do you have an idea on what the benefits of meditation are?

The benefits of meditation

There are multiple benefits of meditation! The one that will catch anybody's eye is the benefit that you will be able to increase your productivity. Through meditation, you will be able to ensure that you are focused in life and are able to achieve what you wanted! This section covers the other benefits of meditation.

The Effect of calm

When you meditate, you are required to clear your mind of all thoughts. You have to ensure that you remove any unwanted thought from your mind. The activity in your brain needs to be minimal when you are meditating. You will find yourself refreshed, like you have woken up from a short nap! There are times when you will find yourself bursting with energy that will last a day!

Helps in increasing your focus

You will find that you are able to focus better in your life when you meditate. You will be able to control your thoughts and your actions with ease. If there is a lot of work that is piling up, you will be able to make sure that every ounce of work is done! If you are a student who has been under a lot of stress, it is good for you to meditate. You will be able to channel your thoughts and focus well on the tasks at hand!

Increasing the functioning of the brain

When you meditate, you will find that you are able to increase the flow of blood into your brain. You will find that the electrical activity in your brain has increased and that you have a good amount of grey matter as well. The added advantage here is that you will be able to ensure that <u>you age slower</u>! That sounds very appealing does it not? You will find yourself with positive thoughts alone!

This chapter helps you understand the best way to heal yourself. You will find that you are able to keep yourself happy even when there are times when the world around you is sad. You can expend your energy to help people keep themselves happy! You will also be able to ensure that you have minimal stress! This is what every person in this fast paced world needs. Irrespective of how you may be on the outside, you could have turmoil of stress inside you. When you meditate, you will find that you are able to keep yourself away from any kind of stress.

There are certain things that you will need to consider when it comes to meditation. This is covered in detail in this chapter.

Instructions

As mentioned above, there are certain things that you will need to keep in mind when you are meditating. You need to ensure that you follow the instructions mentioned below. Only when you do this will you be able to ensure that you are away from stress and any other unhealthy thoughts.

Your surroundings!

Your surroundings play a major role when you are planning

to meditate. This section covers the three main aspects of meditation when it comes to your surroundings:

1. Where you should meditate
2. When should you meditate
3. How do you minimize disturbances if any

Where to meditate

This is the simplest decision that you will have to make! What does anybody who is meditating need most? Silence! You need to ensure that you have a place; either at home or outside, where there is going to be no noise. You have to ensure that the place you choose does not require you to do any other activity; you have to make sure that the place you choose to meditate will need to be clean and tidy. You have to make the effort to clean it occasionally.

When should you meditate

The best time for any person to meditate is the morning. You would have woken up with a good amount of energy. You could also meditate after you have come back from work, but you need to ensure that you are relaxed. If you meditate in the morning, you can be sure that your mind will not wander since you are free from the general thoughts and worries of the day.

It is never a good idea to meditate right after you eat or right before you sleep. You tend to get drowsy. When you meditate before you sleep, you will find that you begin to tolerate a meditation good night's rest. If you do have a problem with sleeping, you could try to meditate before you sleep!

Minimizing disturbances

You may either be living alone or living with family or friends. If you are living alone, there is no question of having any disturbances. But, if your phone disrupts your attention, you will have to ensure that you turn it off when you are meditating. If you are living with friends, sit them down and explain to them what it is that you are doing and why you are doing it. It is always good to communicate. You will be able to ensure that they do not disturb you.

If you are living with family, try to meditate when everybody is asleep or try to meditate when you are alone at home. If you have babies, you could try to meditate when they have gone to bed!

The Posture!

Your posture plays a great role when you are meditating. There are times when bad posture has caused a lot of complications with the back. You may also find yourself feeling drowsy! To ensure that this does not happen, you will need to practice sitting in the position mentioned below. You could also stand or sit on a bench if you find that you cannot sit on the floor. But to stand, you will need to have a good amount of balance in your body. When you meditate, and have succeeded at not having silly thoughts, you will be calm. You may have the feeling that you are flying!

Sitting

When you have chosen to sit down, you could pick sitting on the floor or on a bench or a chair. It is always good to sit on the floor since you will be able to keep yourself upright and in a stable position.

The Floor

Most people prefer sitting on the floor. This is because of the following reasons.

1. You find yourself in a position that is stable. There is no chance of you falling over or hurting yourself. When you have started to meditate well, you will find that you are in a position where you are content with the breath that is in you.
2. You can meditate wherever you want to! This is because you will only have to find a place to sit down! You could go to the park, if you find that the nature around you is what keeps you calm.

Most people tend to sit on a blanket. This is to protect their tailbone. You may strain your tailbone if you do not have a good posture. The section below explains the position that most people sit in.

Standard Position

This is a position that has been passed down from generations. It is a simple position but it would require a good deal of patience from your part.

1. Place the blanket on the floor and sit down on it.
2. Fold your left leg in front of you. You should now place the right leg on top of the left leg. This position is called the '*ardha padmasana*'.
3. Now place your hands on your lap. Place your right palm over the left. Make sure that your palms are facing the ceiling or the sky.
4. The usual position that most people take up is the 'Padmasana'. But it is better if you get used to the ardha padmasana before you get into the padmasana.
5. For the padmasana, you will have to place the left leg on top of the right leg.
6. You have to make sure that your back is straight at all times. You will need to move your hands towards your pelvis or your navel.

7. Make sure that your back is straight at all times.
8. You will now have to close your eyes and <u>focus on your third eye</u>. This is where all your energy is concentrated. There may be times when you start to feel drowsy when you close your eyes. You can leave your eyes half open. If you find that even that is not helping, <u>try to focus on an object</u>. <u>You should make sure that you are only looking at the object and not glaring at it.</u>
9. You have to keep a close eye on your body. You have to make sure that your body stays erect and that you do not slouch. Make sure that you do not sway towards either side. If you find yourself slouching or swaying, you will need to work on relaxing the muscles in that area. You have to ensure that your muscles have gone back to their initial state. Your spine should be taken care of at all times!
10. Once you have mastered the art of sitting straight, you have to ensure that you relax the muscles in your body. You have to first pull your shoulders downward and create an arch between the middle and lower backs. You should pull your stomach in to make sure that you are protecting your spine. You should never let your spine take the entire weight of keeping your body erect.
11. When you are in this posture, you can work on relaxing all the muscles in your body. You have to do this since that is the only way you will be able to ensure that your mind and body do not feel the strain or the stress when you are meditating.

Benches and Chairs

You may have an injury or an illness that prevents you from sitting on the floor. You will not be able to sit on a blanket either. At such times, you could sit on a bench or a chair if you need to. You can sit down on your knees and meditate. There are different kinds of benches available. You have to ensure that you buy the bench that suits you the best!

This makes it very difficult to choose. You will find that you are overwhelmed at the number of benches that are available. You can always switch to sitting on a chair to meditate; you will need to make sure that the chair is not too high. You have to be able to touch the ground with your feet. You will however, not be able to sit in the padmasana or the ardha padmasana pose.

You may be wondering why we have not talked about breathing yet. This the most important part of the meditation process. It needs to be dealt with care.

The Breathing

The way you breathe is very important when it comes to meditation. It is your breath that helps you focus and calm yourself down. This section covers the six simple steps that you can follow to ensure that you are able to breathe well during meditation!

Breathe comfortably

You can do this by taking deep breaths. Every person who has seen you nervous has always told you to take deep breaths. This is because you are able to spread the energy in your body when you breathe in deeply. You will find that you can observe every breath that you take or release when you are meditating. You will find yourself free of negative thoughts when you meditate. This is because of the deep breaths that you take. They tend to cleanse your mind and your body of any negativity.

There is always going to be a difference in the way your body reacts when you begin to meditate. There are times when you will not feel comfortable with the way you are breathing. You will have to try to identify whether or not you are comfortable with the way you breathe during meditation. You can use the steps mentioned below to change your way of breathing if you find that your body is not comfortable with it.

1. You will first need to identify the different parts of your body, which are uncomfortable with the way you are breathing. You will need to channel all your focus on those parts and ensure that they are comfortable with the way you are breathing.
2. You will have to use different patterns of breathing. For instance, you could either take deep breaths or you could choose to breath in and out with forceful breaths. If you find that there is monotony, you will have to be careful with the way your body reacts. Try to identify different ways of breathing to ensure that your body is not comfortable.
3. Try to identify what breath suits the different parts of your body. Also try to see what type of breath your body prefers on the whole!

Concentrate on every breath

When you begin with meditation, you will find your mind wandering around. You will be unable to control your thoughts. It will take some time for you to start focusing your mind. You will have to ensure that you first focus on your breathing and then focus on keeping your mind calm. You will find that your mind wanders no matter how much you try to control it. If it does get out of control, try to think of your breath. If you find that your mind is wandering, control it again. Do this how many ever times you have to!

Observe your breathing and the sensation

You have to begin observing how your body reacts to your breath. You have to begin with your navel since that is where you can identify whether or not you are breathing correctly. Your belly will have to move in and out. Check if your belly is moving in and out. Try to identify how your navel feels when you are taking deep breaths… If there are areas, which are sensitive to your breathing, identify what type of breathing suits it. Continue this with the rest of your torso.

You could begin by spending a little time with the different parts above your waist. You could see how the different parts react towards the different types of breathing. You could then work on spending time with each of these parts to ensure that your body is free of negativity and is calm.

Select your focus spot

People are usually asked to focus on their third eye or the center of their forehead when they meditate. This is because the energy in your body is focused on this spot. This energy is free and flows as commanded by you. When you are meditating, you will have to work on focusing on every part of your body. You will have to focus on your eyes, on your nose, mouth and your breastbone. You could decide to make any of these areas the focus spot. If you are just beginning to meditate, you will not be able to choose the part that works best as the focus spot. You could always experiment with the different parts to see which one works as the best spot!

Spread the awareness throughout your body

Let us consider the example of a flashlight. You may have entered the basement in your house, and have turned the flashlight on. Do you see how far the light from the flashlight spreads? This is how you will have to spread the awareness in your body. This awareness is with respect to your breath. You have to spread the awareness throughout your body through your focus spot. You will have to convince your body that all of it is breathing and not just the focus spot.

Allow the breath to course through you

You have to focus on all the energy that is associated with every breath that you take in when you are meditating. You have to identify if there is a harmony between the energy that is in your body and the breath that you have taken. You have to remember that you have to only focus on your breathing when you are meditating. This has to be done depending on the amount of energy that you have in your body. But this is something that you do not have to worry about. You could let the energy flow like it normally does throughout your body. There are times when you may stop breathing. You do not have to worry about this since your body will now have learnt how to breathe even when you are not. This will only happen when your body is aware of your every breath.

Chapter 11 – Healing Through Yoga

Exercise is the best form of a stress buster. You could heal yourself easily. You will be able to channel your energy and your feelings. This will help you stay calm and healthy. You will find that you are able to rid your mind off its negativity.

Yoga is the best form of exercise. You will be able to breathe well. You will also be able to heal your mind and your body as and when required. This chapter covers certain exercises that you can use to heal yourself. Yoga helps in improving the flow of breath in your body. This flow is what keeps all the negativity at bay. You will find that you are able to learn to breathe in ways that help your channels open up. This helps in spreading a good amount of energy throughout your body.

The Reclining Bound Angle
This exercise is difficult in the beginning. The advantage of this exercise is that you will learn a new way of breathing. You will have to take short breaths when you are performing this exercise. The added advantage is that you will find

yourself energized at the end of the exercise.

Procedure
1. Keep your back straight while sitting on the yoga mat
2. Make sure that your feet are stretched out in front of you
3. Keep your back arched and tuck your chin into your chest
4. Make sure that your hands are either at your sides or are placed on top of your thighs
5. Slightly bend your knees
6. You have to move your knees towards your body.
7. Slowly move your heels towards your pelvic region.
8. Make sure that the soles of your feet are pressed together.
9. Try to bend your knees as far to the side as you can.
10. You can now lean back on your elbows.
11. You have to lower yourself onto the mat.
12. You can use your hands to help you move carefully.
13. You will have to take a short breath and move your hand back above your head into the prayer position.
14. Try to stretch your back by moving your buttocks into a comfortable position.
15. Give your body a chance to find a way to relax itself.
16. Move your knees back into their original position by taking short breaths. Breathe continuously.
17. You will have to breathe in short gusts since that will keep you comfortable throughout this exercise.
18. Take short deep breaths and slowly move out of the position. Try to focus the breath on different parts of your body.
19. You will now have to roll onto your side
20. Make sure that you sit up in a comfortable position.

Corpse Pose

This pose is the easiest of all the yoga poses every! You will be able to identify the best type of breath that you will need while meditating.

Procedure

1. Take deep breaths and lie down on the mat.
2. Your feet have to be kept hip width apart.
3. Keep your hands relaxed and closed to your sides. Try to focus your breath on them and relax them.
4. Keep your palms facing the ceiling
5. Close your eyes and begin to focus your attention and your breath on the different parts of your body. Make sure that you identify the breath that suits the different parts of your body
6. Once you have identified the best breathing style, you have to focus on the flow of the breath throughout your body.
7. You have to see how good the flow of breath is. Check if your breath is coursing through your body from the head to the tip of your toe.
8. Make sure that you stay in this position for as long as you can.
9. Try not to fall asleep! You can use this pose when you are working on the self – hypnosis method of healing!

Surya Namaskar

This exercise is the best exercise in Yoga. You learn how to breathe in this exercise. You need to take long, deep breathes when you are performing this exercise. When you do this, you are letting your body be filled with an immense amount go energy.

Procedure

1. Stand with your back straight on a yoga mat. You have to make sure that there are no gaps between your feet.
2. Make sure that your weight is balanced equally on both feet.
3. Expand your chest with every breath you take!
4. Relax your shoulders while breathing in and out.
5. Take a deep breath in and while releasing the breath move your hands in front of your chest in the prayer position.
6. Slowly release your breath.
7. Take in a deep breath and while releasing it, move your arms upward.
8. Make sure that your biceps are curled towards your ears
9. You have to stand on the tip of your toes and stretch your body.
10. When you feel the pull in your body, take a deep breath in and slowly move backward jutting your pelvis to the front while releasing your breath.
11. This is the step that will help you stretch your spine and exercise the muscles.
12. Breathe out and move back into the standing position.
13. When you are standing erect take a deep breath in and release the breath slowly while bending to touch the floor.
14. Make sure that you breathe out slowly while making your palms touch the floor.
15. Make sure that your knees are not bent. Take another deep breath in and let it out slowly.
16. Try to push your right leg as far back as you can.
17. You have to move your right knee towards the floor.
18. Start looking up and make sure that you are staring straight ahead.

19. Make sure that your left foot is in between your palms. Make sure that you are breathing in and out deeply.
20. Ensure that your body is in a straight line with your arms perpendicular to your body.
21. While exhaling, move your knees to the front
22. Move your hips slightly to the back
23. Start moving lower and make sure that your chin touches the floor.
24. You have to make sure that your buttocks and your tailbone are raised.
25. You have to slowly move into the cobra pose. You will be able to ensure that your hands are holding up your body. You can now begin to lower your chest onto the mat.
26. Your elbows have to be bent
27. You have to make sure that your shoulders are nowhere close to your ears
28. Take a deep breathe in and slowly breathe out.
29. Shift your hips and your tailbone towards the ceiling.
30. Make sure that you lower your chest slowly to the ground. You should ensure that you do not hurt your arms or your back.
31. You have to move your right foot between your palms and stretch your left leg to the back.
32. You need to breathe out slowly.
33. You have to shift your left foot forward
34. You have to now move slowly into the initial position.
35. You have to raise your arms above your head and stretch yourself. When you are stretching yourself take a deep breath in. When you relax breathe out slowly.
36. You can now move your hands to your side and relax your body by taking deep breaths.

Section 3: The Unconventional Methods Of Healing

As mentioned above, there are quite a few methods used to heal one. There are many conventional methods of healing such as meditation, yoga, and sometimes even medication. Apart from these conventional methods, there are certain methods that are not used often by the people to heal themselves! But these methods have shown positive results every time that they have been tried on people. The different methods of healing that have been mentioned in this section are healing you through the law of attraction, healing using the chakras, crystal healing, healing through the aura and healing through self – hypnosis!

Chapter 12 – Healing Through The Law Of Attraction

Before getting into the details of how to heal you through the law of attraction, let us try to understand what the law is.

The law of attraction controls the energy that is found in the universe. It is the law that has declared that all like energy attracts like energy. The universe is full of an energy that vibrates continuously. It does not stay in one place. It is like the tooth fairy from 'Rise of the Guardians'. Just like the tooth fairy, the energy cannot stay in one place. There are times when we believe that we can see and interpret what is happening in the world. But, this is energy at its work! Your thoughts and your actions are all energy. It is just that they vibrate at a different energy level when compared to the energy around us. Your fear and anger vibrate at a very low energy when compared to your joy or your happiness.

There is a new school of thought, which has three main principles of which the Law of Attraction is one. This law always works towards finding an energy that matches your thoughts. If you are a person who has always dreamt of positive things in life, the law of attraction will work towards helping you achieve it! This law works in the very same way with negative energy. The Law is based on the belief that the thought that human beings have been made of pure energy. This energy is what can attract the like energy towards it.

It is only when you begin to understand the law that you will know how you can use it to your benefit. The law states that you will be able to achieve what you desire most in your everyday life. This only happens when you believe that your wish or your desire is true. People have the belief that they will always get what they WANT or what they WISH for. But the truth is that you never get it unless it is yours. You may have come across the saying 'If you love someone, set them free. If they come back to you, they will be yours forever'. This is the case in every area in your life. You will always be able to obtain what you truly believe or desire!

Your thoughts and your energy are what send the world a signal that you have a certain demand. You will be able to ensure that your desires come to life. It is exactly how it sounds!

The advantage here is that the law of attraction will always give you what you want as long as you pay a good amount of attention to it. You could use this law to heal your body and your mind with ease! However, you will need to practice a great deal to ensure that you are able to achieve what you truly desire. It is true that you can heal yourself just by thinking or visualizing it! Your miracle will come true! You will be able to create a life that you want most through the law of attraction. This only happens when you have worked towards harnessing your wishes towards the good of yourself and to others. You will find yourself achieving wonders! You will also be able to ensure that you are completely healed!

You will have to also learn a little about a law called the law of manifestation. The law of manifestation is what helps to ensure that your wishes have been sent out to the universe. The law of attraction is solely dependent on the law of manifestation for it's functioning. There are two secrets behind the law. These secrets are what you can use to ensure that you are able to obtain what you need most.

The Secrets behind the law of attraction

These secrets can be used to heal you. There is an exercise that is mentioned after each secret. You can use this exercise as a blueprint and heal yourself effectively. You could use these methods without any worry. They are very easy to follow too!

Method 1: Ask – Believe – Receive

This is the secret that has been told to people all across the world! There are people all over the world who believe that they can achieve what they want most just by asking. It is true that this secret has helped many people achieve what they want. However, they have needed to practice before. As a person who is just beginning to use the law of attraction to heal yourself, you find that you are able to heal yourself faster and leave a lasting impression. You can always use this method to help you achieve what you want most. But you will only be able to heal yourself if you are able to focus all of your energy!

Ask

If there is something that you have always desired, healing yourself, you have to just ask the universe. Let us assume that you had a terrible pain in your stomach. You would either go take a nap to forget the pain or take a medicine to ease the pain. If it is worse, you go to the doctor and ask him to give you medicines so you can ease the pain. This is what you must do when to comes to the universe. You have to ask the universe what you need most. You should avoid giving the universe any orders. Ask it politely what you need. You will need to first accept the pain and then ask the universe what you desire. You will need to focus all the energy that you have into the request!

Believe

This is the hardest step of all! You need to tell yourself that the pain will go away soon! You need to convince yourself to think that way! This is the only way you will be able to convey to the universe that you need the pain to go away. *Be Gone!* You will have to ensure that you do this in order to get the pain healed. The universe will not give you a pain relief medicine. It is not passed on to you like the heirlooms in your family! You will be able to tell yourself that what you desire most will be given to you only when the time is right. You will be able to believe the idea that you WILL be given what you want most!

Receive

When you are in school or in college, you always gain information that you are open to receiving. This is something that does not happen to every human being. Most human beings are afraid to open their hearts or their minds. You have to let all your fears go since you will only be able to gain what you desire most from the universe if you open your mind! You have to let the universe send you signs and messages in any form it chooses to. It is only when you do this that you receive what you truly need.

You have to remember that what you gain in life is all because of the law of attraction. You may find yourself with no pain at all when you tell yourself that you are absolutely fine. You will find yourself without any stress if that is what you believe in most. You will be able to define to the universe what it is that you truly need and if there is a way to achieve it.

Exercise

Let us now conduct a small exercise.

Assume that you are under too much stress at work. You have begun to have tension headaches and find yourself angry and depressed. This is having a very adverse effect on your mind and your body. You have begun to find it difficult to sleep too! Here is what you can do in such a situation.

1. You have to accept that you are under stress. There are people who can go on with their life even with the headaches. They pop an aspirin and try to push the pain away. You must never do this. You have to accept the fact that you have a pain and let the universe know that you are ready for the treatment.
2. You have to now believe that you will be able to get rid of the pain and the stress. This is the hardest step for you. But you will need to tell yourself that you are going to be cured of the stress.
3. You have to keep yourself open to receiving any signals from the universe. It could be in the form of a new PA or an increase in your pay. You will find yourself feeling better as time passes.
4. Make sure that you continue to believe in the fact that you will have very little stress in the future in order to ensure that you will be able to find a solution!

DESIRE – VISUALIZE – EMOTIONALISE

This is a tricky method to use! But, it is very effective. You will need to have a good amount of practice to ensure that this method works effectively for you. You will find that you are able to achieve what you truly deserve since you will be under the assumption that you have already achieved it! If you are in pain and looking to get help from the universe, you will need to ensure that you are under the assumption that the universe has already cured you. You could use the method mentioned above on a regular basis since it is simple. But this method is more effective when compared to the first one!

You do not have to learn a lot to benefit from using this method. The only thing you will need to do is to ensure that you understand what the method entails. You have to understand the concept and also see what you will need to do in order to achieve what you desire through this method.

DeVisE is an acronym that stands for the method that you are about to undertake. You will need to Devise, Visualize, and Emotionalize. If you follow this acronym word for word, you will be able to ensure that you heal yourself effectively! You need to ASSUME that you have already been healed in order to be noticed by the universe! The last part of this section contains a small exercise that will help you understand how to use this method to heal yourself.

Desire

Let us assume for a second that you have gone to the doctor for a check - up. You have been having terrible headaches and you have been waiting to rule out any disease. You had gone to the doctor a few days ago and had conducted a lot of tests. You have just arrived from work and find an envelope with the hospital's emblem on it. You could either stay calm or give yourself a fright! When you open it and find that there is nothing wrong, you will probably jump around with joy! If you find that there is something wrong, you will be depressed. But let us assume that all is well! You will want to go out for a walk! You will be very relieved. You may be excited that there is nothing wrong with you and jump around with joy. You may begin to act like a little kid on Christmas! You will need to be this little kid when you are trying to ensure that you heal yourself through this method!

When you find yourself wishing for something that heals you, and you KNOW that you will be happy, you will need to work towards believing in it! You should never show fake excitement since that will never give you the best results. If you find yourself hoping that you heal, you will need to obsess about it. You have to ensure that you are able to give signs to the universe that you are ready to be healed. This is the best way to ensure that the Law of Attraction works in your favor!

Visualize

You have identified the fact that you want a report that says that you are absolutely fine! You will need to act like the report only contains that information since that will help you convince yourself that you have a clean report! You will have to find the excitement and the happiness that you would feel if you had the report in your hand. You have to believe that you have ALREADY RECEIVED it. You have to believe in the past tense!

When you find that you have it, you have to make sure that your body knows that you have it! You have to feel all that you would if you genuinely had it!

Emotionalize

This is the last step in this method, which will help you make the law of attraction work for you. You have already convinced yourself that you have what you are asking from the universe. You have to now show the universe how you would feel if you have received all that you have asked for! You have to show the universe how you will feel if you have received a clean report! When you find yourself in this state, you will feel gracious towards the universe. You will praise God and also find ways to thank him!

You will need to act this way since you have convinced yourself that you have what you need most! Since you have let yourself believe that you already have it, you will find it very easy to feel the way you would if you actually had it! You have to show the universe how grateful you are towards it.

You have to master all three steps that have been mentioned in this method. It is only when you master these steps that you will be able to ensure that you achieve what you desire most. You need to show the universe that you need it! You have to give it all you have in order to ensure that the universe believes that you need what you are asking for!

Before you begin this method you will need to distinguish between your wishes and your wants. It is a known fact that you never get what you wish for. There are only a few times when you will be given what you want most by the universe. There are times when you will never get it. Let us assume that you have indigestion in your stomach. You will want the universe to help you get rid of it. You can guarantee that this is something that can be cured very easily. You will have to believe that it can be cured.

If you really want something, you have to let the universe

know that you desperately need it. Only then will you get what you desire most! You have to let the universe know that you will get it, but you are unsure of when that may happen. This is a feeling that leaves you with a sense of calm as opposed to the feeling where you will tell yourself that you will never get what you deserve. You are now in the state where your wish has reached the universe and will manifest itself soon!

You will need to have immense faith when it comes to using this method to heal yourself. You will have to constantly believe that you are able to achieve what you desire most! You need to tell yourself that you are able to get what you NEED and not what you WANT. This universe works towards giving you what you need. You will be able to communicate with the universe on a regular basis and tell it what you need. This can only be done when you believe and visualize the idea that you have ALREADY been relieved from the pain that you have been feeling!

Exercise

You have covered the basic ways by which you will be able to ensure that you can achieve what you desire most. Let us assume that you have just been to the doctor since you have found yourself feeling uneasy. You have visited the psychiatrist and have told him that you feel low on many occasions on account of the fact that you live alone. You have told the psychiatrist that you need to have a person by your side at all times. This is the only way you can live. You have always dreamt of finding the person who will stick by you through thick or thin. You have lost your mind trying to find such a person. You have become very uneasy. You need to know whether there is a person out there for you. You could use this method.

1. You have to work towards believing that you are going to find the person very soon. You will need to keep thinking this in order to ensure that the universe has understood that you need someone.
2. You will have to tell the universe that you already have it. You will have to act the way you would if you already had the person. You would be happy and carefree. You would find yourself singing to the music on the streets! You will need to let the universe know how exactly you would feel if you found the person.

You will have to be gracious towards the universe for giving you what you need most! It is only then that you will get what you deserve most.

Chapter 13 – Healing Through Chakras

The chakras are the different parts of your body where there is a greater concentration of energy. There are major and minor chakras in our body. The major chakras are where the energy is concentrated at a higher level. The minor chakras aid the major chakras in keeping the energy at a stable level in the body. This chapter provides you with the information on the major chakras and the tips on how to cure the imbalances in those chakras.

The Major Chakras

There are seven major chakras in the human body and numerous minor chakras. This section of the chapter deals with the different chakras and the colors that will suit them.

The Root Chakra

This is the first chakra in the entire body and is the main chakra! It is found at the base of your spine and is very close to the tailbone. This chakra is associated with the color red. This chakra deals with relationships. It defines our relationships with our families and friends. This chakra is also responsible for any pleasure, pain, sexuality and survival instincts.

The Sacral Chakra

This chakra is the second chakra in the body. This is located below the navel and right above the pelvic region. The chakra is associated with the color orange. This chakra is linked to the right side of your brain. It is related to your creativity, your playfulness and your feelings.

The Solar Plexus

The third chakra, or the solar plexus, is the longest chakra. It moves from the navel to the heart. This chakra is associated with the color yellow. This chakra gives you your individuality. You will be able to assess your self – worth and also understand your ego better.

The Heart Chakra

The fourth chakra is called the heart chakra. This chakra is located at the center of your chest between your ribs. It is associated with the colors green and pink. This chakra defines your spirituality and your ability to love. You will find your inspiration through this chakra. You will learn to be confident if this chakra is always balanced.

The Throat Chakra

The fifth chakra is called the throat chakra. This is located at the base of your throat. This oIt is located at the base of the throat. It is mainly associated with the color blue. This chakra is associated with your ability to make decisions. You will identify your level of authority. This chakra ensures that you speak the truth and that you surrender to being who is superior to you.

The Brow Chakra

The sixth chakra is called the brow chakra. This is the focus spot in most meditation classes. This is often referred to as the third eye chakra. This chakra lies between the eyebrows in the middle of the forehead. This chakra is associated with indigo. It tells you about your level of intelligence. It talks about your wisdom too!

The Crown Chakra

The last chakra, called the crown chakra lies at the top of the head. It lies at the part of your head, which is called the crown. This chakra is associated with your devotion and your ability to inspire and be inspired. The color associated with this chakra is violet.

How to clear the imbalances within the chakras

This section deals with the different ways to heal the different chakras. If the energy in your chakras is imbalanced, you will find that you have begun to doubt yourself. The imbalances have to be treated immediately.

The Root Chakra

This chakra is very dense and has a lot of energy in it. When you are looking at healing the chakra, you will have to work on physical exercises. This chakra is related to your sense of smell. It is always a good idea to remove the imbalances through aromatherapy or meditation with aroma. The different earth elements like gemstones are very effective. They have been known to heal and balance this chakra effectively. You could also try hatha yoga when you are trying to balance the energy in the chakra.

The Sacral Chakra

The second chakra is dense too. It is however, not as dense as the first chakra. But since it is dense, you could use similar therapies that you used to balance the first chakra. Physical activities are the best option to clear out any imbalances. You could try tantric yoga to balance this chakra. There are different foods that you could consume to ensure that you heal this chakra. These are covered in the next section of the chapter. This is because this chakra is related to the sense of taste. The chakra is associated with the element water. Any water element can be used to balance this chakra.

The Solar Plexus Chakra

This chakra is the one that is related to your self – image. You determine your worth based on the views of this chakra. Visual therapies are the way to go to heal this chakra. You could use affirmations and yantra to heal the chakra. This chakra is closely related to fire. You could use elements of fire to ensure that you heal this chakra. You could pursue an outdoor activity or go sunbathing!

The Heart Chakra

This chakra is the bridge between the physical and spiritual chakras. This chakra connects the chakras that lie below it and above it. The best way to clear this chakra of any imbalances is through meditation. You could also use crystal healing for this chakra. This is covered in the last chapter of the book. You could also go for massages. This chakra is related to air and the best way to clear the imbalance is through breathing exercises and meditation.

The Throat Chakra

This chakra is the one that is related to sounds. The best way to heal this chakra would be to use the element of sound. You could use different kinds of music. You could also chant certain hymns and verses. This will restore the balance in the chakra. You could use your favorite song or use the different utensils in your house to make music.

The Third-Eye Chakra

This chakra is the one that gives you the ability to look inside yourself. You could have inner vision through this chakra. The best way to ensure that this chakra is balanced is through meditation. You could also use affirmations!

The Crown Chakra

This chakra directly deals with the knowledge and the form of conscience. You can only heal this chakra through meditation. This has been explained in Chapter 10 of this book!

Healing Foods

As mentioned above, there are different foods that can be consumed by you to heal the chakras. You have to remember that there are certain foods that have a different effect on the different chakras. This section covers the foods that you could consume in order to heal yourself and balance your chakras.

The Root Chakra

This chakra helps in keeping you grounded. You will find that you are connected to the earth. The best foods to boost this chakra are proteins from animals, mushrooms, food that is red in color since this chakra is associated with red. You could also have root vegetables since they come from the earth and have a direct affinity towards earth.

The Sacral Chakra

This chakra is associated with your creativity. You will need to ensure that this chakra is balanced. Only if it is balanced will it ensure that your creativity enters this world in some form. You can consume fats, oils, and food that are orange in color!

The Solar Plexus Chakra

The third chakra gives you power when it is balanced. You feel helpless when there is an imbalance in the chakra. The foods that can be consumed to balance the chakra are fiber, carbs, yellow colored foods such as corn and legumes among many more.

The Heart Chakra

The heart chakra helps you love yourself and the people around you. If this chakra is imbalanced, you will find yourself disliking you and the world around you. There are certain foods that you could consume to heal this chakra. You could eat broccoli, cabbage, kale and other food that is rich in chlorophyll. This is because this chakra is associated with the color green.

The Throat Chakra

When you have a balanced throat chakra, you will find that you are able to communicate your emotions with ease. You find it easier to express your emotions. If this is imbalanced, you will find it difficult to talk to people. The foods that heal this chakra are sauces, juices and plants from the sea. The best combination of food would be the one that has a bit of the element of water and earth.

The Third Eye Chakra

The third eye chakra deals with your dreams. You are able to follow a divine guide because of this chakra. You will find that you have no faith in the universe or a higher power if this chakra is imbalanced. You can consume tea, coffee, wine and fruits and vegetables that have a violet tinge in them. *example?*

The Crown Chakra

A crown chakra that is healthy will help you manifest the belief that there is a super power out there. You will be able to ensure that you obtain a good amount of knowledge. You cannot associate this chakra with any food since this chakra does not have a specific function. The best medication for this chakra would be sunlight, water and air.

Chapter 14 – Healing Through Self – Hypnosis

Most people have heard of what hypnosis is. They know that there are people out there who could hypnotize you and make you do what they want you to do. Did you know that hypnosis is used to help a person cure himself? You can change a person's habits and characteristics if you hypnotize him. Not every person out there is comfortable with letting a person decide how he must be. They would rather never experience a session on hypnosis. But you need not fear! You could hypnotize yourself! Do not worry about it. This chapter provides you with a four-week plan to help you master self – hypnosis. You will find that you are able to make changes to your behavior with ease.

You should remember that there is no specific time when you have to perform hypnosis on yourself. The only prerequisite is that there must be a quiet place! You would not need more than half an hour to conduct this session.

The Four-Week Program!

This section covers the different steps that you will have to take when you are learning to heal yourself through self – hypnosis.

Week 1 *Task about notes first!*

This is the simplest week of all! You will have to meditate in a particular manner to ensure that you are relaxed.

1. You will have to first sit in a relaxed position.
2. Make sure that you are free for the next half an hour. Ensure that you do not have your mobile phone with you.
3. Find a spot on the wall above you and fix your eyes to it! Make sure that you do not move your gaze away from that point for the next five minutes.
4. You will have to take a deep breath and count backwards from 5 to 1. You will need to repeat this very step 10 times.
5. On the last '1' you will need to convince yourself that your eyes are heavy and that you have to close them. You are only doing this because you are allowed to. There are times when you may need music to help you get into the groove. Please choose music that you will like.
6. You can now take five minutes to work on relaxing your body. You will have to start from the head to the tip of your toes.
7. You will find that you have begun to relax. When you find that you have finally relaxed, you could tell yourself that you are strong – physically and mentally. You should also remember that this process ensures that you become more confident.

8. You can now finally open your eyes! Take a deep breath and open your eyes. You will find that you have relaxed.

You may wonder why this is given a week to master. It does seem easy, but it is tough since you have to get your mind to relax.

Week 2

When you enter week 2, you will realize that you have begun n to relax yourself sooner! You do not require a half hour to relax yourself.

1. This week is where you will have to identify the area where you would like to concentrate. This could be either a personal or a professional problem. You will be able to heal yourself.
2. You will have to give yourself a boost! Give yourself positive suggestions – they could just be words. These are what give you the boost to push yourself forward! This step does not take more than fifteen to twenty minutes. *Example of positive suggestions*

Week 3

You have made notes for yourself. These notes have to be the ones that you made during the first week. *What?*

1. Find your spot and fix your eyes on the spot. Focus only on the spot. You will need to hold your notes in your hands between the focus point and your eyes.
2. You will have to read the suggestions to yourself. Repeat each suggestion at least ten times.
3. Now place your notes away from you. You can now pay attention to the spot on the ceiling.
4. Begin to take deep breaths ad start counting backwards from 5 to 1.

5. The minute you reach the final count one, you have to close your eyes.
6. You will need to relax your body like you did during the first week.
7. Once that is done, you will have to repeat the suggestions that you made for yourself repeatedly.
8. You should do this for the next two minutes.
9. In the next five minutes, you will have to tell yourself that you are great. You have to repeat this proves. Make sure that you try to relax yourself faster each time.
10. Once you are done, you can count from 1 to 5 and open your eyes.

Week 4

This is the final week! You will be able to hypnotize yourself successfully!

1. Move into a very comfortable position.
2. You will need to repeat the steps that have been mentioned in the third week.
3. Your body has now been conditioned to listen to you. You will realize that you are now directly moving into a state of hypnosis without any preamble.

How to develop suggestions for the third week

This is an important step! You have to be very careful with how you develop suggestions since that is what decides whether or not you are going to change your habit or not! This section covers a few suggestions that you could use for yourself. The situation is given in the bracket next to the suggestion. If you are going through such a problem, you could heal yourself through self – hypnosis using the suggestions mentioned below. But before that, there are certain things that you have to keep in mind.

1. You have to make sure that you are optimistic. You need to make sure that your suggestions are all positive. This is to ensure that every suggestion that you make will create a greater impact since it is a positive suggestion.
2. You have to ensure that your suggestions are all time bound. Make sure that they are placed in the immediate future. Never say 'Quit smoking'. It does not say by when you have to quit smoking.
3. You have to make sure that you have simple and direct suggestions. This is to ensure that your subconscious accepts the suggestions that have been made.
4. You have to try and relate your suggestions to any achievement that you would have had in the past regarding the same suggestion. This will help you reinforce the likelihood of success.

Examples of suggestions

This section covers certain examples of suggestions that you could use.

1. I will always be satisfied with one snack a day – this could be a suggestion for a person who is fighting obesity.
2. I will never be tempted to smoke even if there are people around me who smoke – this is for a person who wants to quit smoking
3. I will be motivated to study much more when I enter the classroom – a student who finds it very difficult to concentrate in class
4. When I hear someone talking to me, I will be able to comprehend what they are saying without any

difficulty – this is a suggestion for a person who has problems with comprehension
5. I will be able to remember whatever I have read and listened to easily – a person with the lack of memory
6. I will ensure that I remain calm about my performance in an examination when I sit down to write the examination – fear of examinations
7. I am going to be a very confident person with a good capability to do my work. I will be self – assured and feel worthy of myself in every part of my life – a person who lacks self – confidence
8. I will make sure that I abide by the deadlines that have been set for me. I will make sure that I do not leave an assignment to the last day – a person who procrastinates.

Chapter 15 – Healing Using Crystals

Crystals have been used for a very long time for healing. They have been used since the ancient times for healing. There are different kinds of crystals that are found all over the world. In order to use a crystal to heal yourself, you have to ensure that the crystal you have chosen is perfect for you. This will only happen if you have certain knowledge about the crystal. However, there is an easier approach. You can choose your own crystal by going by your gut. When you enter a store and are looking at buying a crystal, all you have to do is stay calm and hold out your hand. The crystal that shows an affinity towards you is the crystal that is perfect for you. There are different ways in which a crystal can be used to heal you.

General Healing Methods

There are some general uses for a crystal. This section covers the different methods that have been used over the ages to heal a person's mind and body.

Worn on the body

There are many people who have benefited from a crystal when they have worn them. There are people who have benefitted from the properties of the crystal when they have held them close to their bodies. There are people who will always pick the crystal that has a positive effect on them. They do this when they do not know how to pick crystals.

The main point to note is that the place where the crystal lies also plays a major role! If the crystal lies at the base of the throat or at the throat chakra, it will affect all the organs that are related to the throat chakra. This does not mean that the other organs do not benefit. But, the greater effect of the chakra is on the organs controlled by the throat chakra.

Placed under a Pillow

There are multiple advantages to placing your crystals under your pillow when you go to bed. You would be able to ensure that you have no nightmares. You will also have no problems with sleeping. You could keep insomnia at bay! There are certain crystals that can be used to ensure that you do not forget your dreams.

While Meditating

The crystals have a certain vibration of energies within themselves. These vibrations often calm the mind down. When you are meditating, you can hold the crystal in your hand or in front of you. This way you will be able to ensure that you do not have too many thoughts and are able to calm yourself down.

There are other techniques that require a certain amount of practice. These techniques have been developed by the ages by different people. This section covers a few techniques that have been developed and used.

Crystal healing techniques

Crystal Pendulum

This technique can be used to re-energize your body. Through this technique any imbalances in your body's energy on a spiritual, metal [mental] and a physical level are removed.

Procedure

- Ask the patient to lie down comfortably. [What is a neutral swing?]
- Ensure that there is no disturbance in the area; make sure that the surroundings are quiet.
- Sit next to the patient. Make sure that you are relaxed too.
- You will need to hold the pendulum between your thumb and your fore finger. Make sure that you are holding it very loose.
- Make sure that your hand and your body are relaxed
- You now suspend the pendulum at the patient's feet and start moving upward. You have to oscillate the pendulum. This swing of the pendulum is called the neutral swing.
- Slowly move up towards the head from the feet. When you find the pendulum oscillating in a different manner, stay there till the pendulum starts to oscillate in the neutral swing.
- Once you reach the top of the head, you will have to go back and repeat the process. Move along the sides of the body and clear out the imbalances wherever you can find them.

Crystal Wand

This technique is used to re-energize the energy systems of your body. They remove all the negative energies and the tensions that you have been facing.

Procedure
- Ask the patient to lie down comfortably.
- Ensure that there is no disturbance in the area; make sure that the surroundings are quiet.
- Lower yourself next to your patient. Make sure that you are comfortable too.
- Move the wand from the feet to the head.
- Make clockwise movements at the feet. Now slowly move upward.
- If you find that the wand has become heavy or if it changes motion, it means that you have to change the movement of the wand. You can change the movement to balance the energy but change the movement right back to the beginning.
- Now that you have reached the top of the head, you will have to move the wand in the reverse direction. Make the same small circles!
- This method helps recharge the body's energy fields.

Crystal Healing Layout

A crystal-healing layout is the technique where you surround yourself with crystals! These are different crystal. This type of healing is commonly called a crystal healing.

This layout has a very strong electromagnetic field. This field works at healing your entire body. At times you could focus the energy to heal a certain part of the body. It helps in clearing out the imbalances in the energy system. All the fields in your body will be aligned. This is due to the changes made to the energy in your system.

You will instantly find a difference. You will find that your chakras are healed and balanced. You will be able to stay away from illnesses and diseases. If they were manifesting your body, they were gone when you cleansed yourself.

There are different layouts for different people. The chakras in people are at different levels leading to a different layout. You cannot expect to have the same layout as anybody else! Only the healer will know the layouts.

Figure Eight Looping

This technique is perfect to remove the imbalances in your chakra and also try to align them. You will have to make the figure eight using the different crystals for each chakra. You will need to make the figure eight using these crystals.

Procedure

- You will need to understand your patient well
- Try to know where his chakras lie exactly.
- Make sure that the patient is lying down comfortably. Ensure that the surroundings are quiet
- You will need to seat yourself at the side of your patient. You will have to ensure that you are comfortable too!
- You must now begin arranging the crystals in the order of the chakra. You will have to ensure that you are aligning the chakras.
- When the patient has calmed himself down, he will begin to feel the effect of the crystals on the different chakras and find a calm spreading through his body. This indicates that his chakras are aligning themselves.

Tracing the Meridians

In order to make this technique an effective method of treatment, you will have to know what an acupressure point is. You also have to have the knowledge of a meridian line. You will need to understand their importance and also the need for the lines and the points. When you understand the importance you will be able to ensure that your patients are all healed. You will not have to worry about doing it wrong. However, if you do not have a fair knowledge, refrain from performing this technique.

This process is long and tedious. It requires you to have prior knowledge of the acupressure points. It is also required for you to know your patient well.

Procedure
- Ask the patient to lie down comfortably.
- Ensure that there is no disturbance in the area; make sure that the surroundings are quiet.
- Make sure that you have the list of acupressure points of your patient.
- After your patient has become comfortable, you should sit next to the patient.
- Using the crystal that will work for your patient, you should press all the acupressure points and the line that joins them. These lines are called the meridian lines. Make sure that you do not miss a point.

Your patient may have a preference for a gemstone. The ideal stone to use would be the quartz point. But you have to put the patient first since he knows what he wants.

Conclusion

Throughout this book, I have given you examples to try and explain in everyday terms what body and mind healing is all about. It isn't about deprivation. It isn't about making yourself into something that you are not. It's about using your body and your mind in harmony and learning the harmonics that keep it in tune. When playing a guitar recently, after learning at a very late stage in life, my hands suddenly started to actually get the notes right automatically. I wasn't thinking about them, nor was I thinking about the mistakes I might make. Instead, I simply listened to the music and let my hands do the rest. The mind body connection was fantastic.

There is the opportunity for everyone to feel well and to live in a really happy lifestyle but many resists it. They are too busy blaming others or blaming their situation on life itself. Each person that enters this life is given an opportunity to shine and it's great to know that you can have a hand in healing your body and in healing the way that the mind thinks rather than passing on the responsibility and blaming something or someone else. When you pass the buck, you don't learn the ways of healing that are open to everyone. There's a wonderful world awaiting you when you start to replace all those negative feelings with new friendships and using your creative and logical processes to actually find enjoyment. There is a whole other world out there when you tell yourself "Something's wrong and I need to do something." Instead of blame, which is in itself negative, you begin to see potential solutions that help keep your life in balance.

The busy and competitive nature of the world is hard to bear sometimes. Sometimes you feel you don't measure up but whose measure are you using? Begin with being happy about whom you are and the measurements change. Don't let your happiness in life be conditional upon living to someone else's rules. You are an individual and how you heal your mind and body depends upon your willingness to change.

Does it make sense to blame the food when you are overweight? Does it make sense to blame the TV when you get a headache? Does it make sense to blame another human being for your own failings? Of course not. The path of life isn't easy at the best of times, but when you learn to play the game of life, you find your own victories in defeating the things that make you suffer. Take time out and meditate, give your mind room for relaxation and your subconscious kicks in with potential solutions. You have the power to heal your mind and to heal your body and even if told that you have the most crippling disease, a healed mind will help you to minimize the damage so that the body illness doesn't detract from who you are. Healing your mind, healing your body and changing your life will make you a stronger person. It will make you a happier person and it will make all the people that share your life happy to have you as part of their lives. Happy people are much more capable of dealing with pain and don't suffer as much as those who bask in their illnesses because they want attention.

If you are wondering if you have the strength to incorporate all of these ideas into your life, the fact that you have read this far tells me that you have. You want change in your life. You want to be able to get up in the morning and be happy. You want to feel the pain both emotional and physical minimized to a manageable level and the system described within this book will allow you to have everything that you need within your life to combat illness, combat pain and change your whole approach to life.

The power lies in your own hands. The power lies in your thought patterns, the way you allow your body to rest and relax, how you feed it and how you work your way through your problems, allowing yourself time for creative activities as well. When the right side of your brain works in conjunction with the left, and your mind is able to feel a real connection with your body through relaxation and meditation, you begin to realize that we are each in control of our own quality of life. When a child wakes up in the morning and greets the world with awe, that's what we lose as we get older. You can rediscover that awesome feeling of wonder when you follow your dreams, and it may well be worth reading through the book another time, while you put all of the steps shown herein into practice in an effort to maximize the joy in your life and feel the change in every day that awaits you. You will have healed your mind, you will have healed your body and as a consequence, you will also have changed your life.

I hope this book inspires you to discover your own path to wellness and healing.

May God bless you and your life.

In love and wellness,

Mary Solomon

You May Enjoy Mary's Other Book on Healing

HEALING: Heal Your Body Heal Your Life

smarturl.it/healingaa

Other Popular Books By Mary Solomon

Below you'll find some of Mary's other popular books on Amazon.

hyperurl.co/MarySolomon

HEARING GOD'S VOICE FOR BEGINNERS

smarturl.it/heargod

TIBETAN SECRETS: Five Steps To Unlimited Energy And Restored Health

smarturl.it/5rites

CRYSTAL HEALING ENERGY

smarturl.it/crystala

CHAKRA HEALING EXPOSED

smarturl.it/chakraaa

RECOMMENDED READING

Boundaries: Line Between Right And Wrong
hyperurl.co/boundaries

Creativity : Creative Thinking To Improve Memory, Increase Success and Live A Healthy Life

hyperurl.co/creative

SELF ESTEEM: Confidence Building: Overcome Fear, Stress and Anxiety: Self Help Guide

hyperurl.co/selfesteem

Tantric Sex: Couples Guide: Communication, Sex And Healing

hyperurl.co/tantric

Crystals and Gemstones: Healing The Body Naturally

hyperurl.co/crystalgames

Made in the USA
San Bernardino, CA
04 May 2016